World of Difference

Global mission at the pick 'n' mix counter

World of Difference

Global mission at the
pick 'n' mix counter

Richard Tiplady

PATERNOSTER PRESS

First published in 2003 by Paternoster Press

09 08 07 06 05 04 03   7 6 5 4 3 2 1

Paternoster Press is an imprint of Authentic Media,
P.O. Box 300, Carlisle, Cumbria, CA3 0QS, UK
and
P.O. Box 1047, Waynesboro, GA 30830-2047, USA

Website: www.paternoster-publishing.com

British Library Cataloguing in Publication Data
A catalogue record for this book is available from the British Library

ISBN 1-84227-244-6

Cover Design by FourNineZero
Typeset by WestKey Ltd, Falmouth, Cornwall
Printed in Great Britain by Cox & Wyman, Reading, Berkshire

For Irene and Jamie,
who believe in me even when I don't

Contents

Foreword

If the number of books published in the past few years on the subject of Christian mission is anything to go by, reports of the death of the missionary movement have been greatly exaggerated. This present volume is not merely another piece of incidental evidence that missionary concern remains alive and well in the Western world, but rather it constitutes a unique and very significant contribution to the debate concerning the future shape and practice of mission in the context of postmodernity and globalization.

Frankly, I cannot think of anyone better qualified to write this book than Richard Tiplady. The combination of an insider's knowledge of a wide range of missionary organizations, gained through working closely with them over a number of years, and a deep personal engagement with the challenges posed by a changing culture have given the author unique insights which enable him, through this volume, to advance our understanding of the task of mission today in ways that are significantly new.

The strengths of the book are many. It offers a detailed analysis of contemporary culture, which, while based on wide reading from a diversity of sources, is both critical and independent. In particular, this is emphatically not simply another Christian jeremiad lamenting the decline of the West. Rather, what the reader will discover in these pages is a ringing affirmation of the positive opportunities for mission provided by the changes occurring at the present time. However, what makes this book truly unique is its essentially practical concern with models and structures for mission in the new world of the twenty-first century and the guidance and advice it offers in this respect will be invaluable to all who are concerned with mission today.

I have often likened the present situation in mission, in which we find ourselves between an old paradigm that no longer works and a new one that remains unclear, to the experience of attending missionary deputation meetings in which two colour slides became jammed together in the projector. The image on the screen was wonderfully coloured, but utterly incomprehensible! In this book, Richard Tiplady helps us to disentangle those conflicting pictures with the result that the way ahead can be discerned with greater clarity. Not everyone who reads this work will agree with all the claims and proposals made here, nor would the author expect anything other than the stimulation of ongoing discussion and debate. However, there is no doubt that this very readable book advances our understanding of both the context for mission and the theoretical and structural changes that are required for its practice in a globalized world. Moreover, *World of Difference* constitutes evidence that a generation of Christians, who are self-consciously postmodern, are determined to bear witness to the gospel in ways that are both faithful and relevant, and for this the author is to be thanked and God is to be praised.

David Smith
International Christian College, Glasgow

Acknowledgements

I couldn't have done it without you ...

This book is part of the *Connect!* vision developed by Oasis Charitable Trust and now involving other mission agencies with the goal of seeing more local churches directly engaged in effective cross-cultural mission. Mission agencies are no longer the primary stakeholder in the missionary enterprise. But they are still a significant one, and it is my hope that these organizations will continue to play a vital role in the global missionary movement that is getting increasingly close to being 'from everywhere to everywhere'.

Although it sometimes feels like it after long hours spent in front of a computer screen, no book is a solo enterprise. I want to express my deep gratitude to Oasis, without whose generous financial sponsorship this book would not have been written. In particular, my thanks go to Tim Jeffery, Head of Global Action at Oasis, for his inspiration, friendship and searching questions. Ros Johnson provided helpful suggestions and comments throughout the writing process, helping me to clarify meanings and implications.

There are also those who gave their time freely when I sought their opinion on matters raised in this book – David Smith, Jonathan Ingleby, Brian Stanley, Stan Nussbaum, Rose Dowsett, Mark Orr, Tim Chester, Steve Timmis, and

Tom and Christine Sine. Jim Plueddeman, Malcolm McGregor and Stanley Green all kindly took the time to confirm that I had represented their organizations fairly and accurately.

There are also many unnamed contributors to this book, people I have had the privilege of working with or talking with or listening to over the past few years. They have helped to shape my thinking, and I will be pleased if I manage to shape theirs in return.

Richard Tiplady
< www.tiplady.org.uk >
31 March 2003

Chapter 1

Globalization

Not just riots and Coca-Cola

Dateline: June 2002

The first customers arrived at the Café All'Angelo at 3 a.m. yesterday morning. By 4 a.m., still an hour before Italy's game against Croatia, the Italian eaterie in New York's Greenwich Village was bursting with Italian-Americans making another dawn appointment with emotional intensity.

These fans were desperate for a second successive Italian victory in the FIFA World Cup, which would send the Azzurri into the tournament's second round. As the game unfolded, svelte waitresses had to weave through the throng, carrying cups of cappuccino and cornetti filled with zabaglione cream.

Those who had got up obscenely early to follow their team, and those who had not bothered to go to bed, were soon rewarded. A goal early in the second half from Italy's predatory striker Christian Vieri, his third in two games, sent the crowd into ecstasy. But their hopes of World Cup glory quickly turned to pain as two strikes in four minutes by their unfancied opponents handed Croatia a win that ranks alongside the other amazing upsets – Korea beating Poland, the USA toppling much-fancied Portugal – which helped turn this World Cup into probably the best football tournament ever played.

More than 5,000 miles away from New York, scores of inhabitants of Soweto had risen early to crowd round a small TV set to watch South Africa earn a creditable 2–2 draw with Paraguay. They went on to beat Slovenia 1–0. When Senegal vanquished defending champions France 1–0 on the opening day, hundreds of Senegalese danced jigs of joy in front of the Arche de la Défense in Paris at this famous victory over their former colonial masters.[1]

All over the world, billions of people have been watching the most exciting, most popular and most truly international World Cup in history. After decades as an obsession in Europe and South America, but almost nowhere else, the world's most popular sport has finally gone global.

Welcome to the world

Globalization is not something that is often associated with football. Instead, the word usually conjures up images of protest against global economic and trading structures, the unstoppable onward march of the golden arches of McDonald's, the Nike 'swoosh' and dodgy videos on MTV.

We often think of globalization as an economic phenomenon. The riots at the World Trade Organization Seattle meetings in 1999 and the G8 gathering in Genoa in 2001, books like *No Logo*, *The Silent Takeover* and *The Captive State*, along with counter-strikes from economists and business leaders, embody a passionate debate about the nature and source of human prosperity at the beginning of the twenty-first century. The opponents of economic globalization doubt the real motives of corporations that look to

---

[1] This story first appeared in *The Observer*, Sunday 9 June 2002. See < www.observer.co.uk/Print/0,3858,4429900,00.html >.

move production and expand their markets into Majority World countries. Its advocates argue that 'there is no alternative', and that economic globalization can be made to work for the benefit of the poor as well as the rich.

Closely associated with these images of economic globalization is the spread of global brands around the world. Coke, Gap, Nike, McDonald's, Starbucks, MTV ... these and other global brands are associated with the West in the minds of consumers around the world and provide a way for emerging middle classes to identify with and aspire to the Western lifestyle. The corporations behind these brands are only too willing to assist the realization of those aspirations, generously making their branded products available to all who can afford them!

Is it any wonder then that globalization is so easily associated with Westernization (or, more usually, Americanization) and is viewed by many in neo-colonial terms, as Western imperialism in its latest incarnation? The emperor's new clothes might come with a logo on the collar, but sadly the empire is still intact.

Football: the globalized sport?

Football, by contrast, is on the way to becoming a truly global sport. The Republic of Korea surprised many during the 2002 World Cup, managing to defeat some of Europe's strongest national teams, including Portugal, Italy and Spain, in fairly short order. Senegal's opening match victory over world champions France set the tone for a tournament which saw the old order of football, well, not overturned exactly (the final was, after all, between Germany and Brazil), but at least shaken. At times, the emperor looked as though he had been stripped down to his Calvin Kleins.

I do not want to extol the virtues of football as a model for the new world order. Corporations like Nike and Adidas both do very well from the sale of replica shirts and footballs as a result of their sponsorship of the world's elite football players and teams. But we can use it as a way of noting that the free association of globalization with Western global dominance is a bit simplistic, and does not help us to understand the complex nature of the world today, nor its implications for world mission.

I do not believe that globalization is simply about Westernization. It is not a single set of processes built around some economic and political trends. It is not only 'the ever-increasing integration of national economies into the global economy through trade and investment rules and privatisation, aided by technological advances'.[2] It includes some of these things, but it is much more than this.

So what is globalization?

Globalization is something of a hydra. It includes many different phenomena and impacts many different aspects of human life. Trying to come to grips with it is like trying to nail jelly to a wall. As if that wasn't enough, then, like the multi-headed beast of Greek mythology,[3] when you cut off one head (i.e. when you think you have got globalization pinned down and understood), three more heads appear in its place. So we will start with a definition that, however

[2]   Colin Hines, quoted by Ruth Valerio in 'Globalisation and The Poor: Tearfund Policy Paper' < www.globalconnections.co.uk /pdfs/globalization.pdf >.

[3]   The hydra had the body of a dog and 100 serpentine heads. It also had poisonous breath and was so hideous it caused most people to die of fear simply from seeing it. My cat would still have treated it with disdain.

general, provides the basis for building a more detailed understanding and analysis.

> Globalization as a concept refers to both the compression of the world and intensification of consciousness of the world as a whole ... both concrete global interdependence and consciousness of the global whole.[4]

This definition, coined by Roland Robertson in 1992, is helpful in that it is both broad and inclusive, not confining globalization to one part of human life (e.g. economics), and yet at the same time it is concise and brief. So what does it mean?

Geography is history: increasing global interconnectedness

The world is increasingly interconnected. Events and decisions in one part of the world have significant impact on other parts of the world. The Asian financial crises of 1997, which affected the currencies and economies of Thailand, Malaysia, South Korea and Indonesia in rapid succession, leading to recession and unemployment, were triggered in large part by currency speculation in the financial centres of London, New York, Frankfurt and Tokyo. Falling commodity prices can affect the livelihoods of many in the Majority World, as the cash crops they grow for export become worth less than it costs to grow them. Flying jet airliners into skyscrapers in New York can lead to the collapse, a few weeks later, of the governing regime on the other side of the world implicated in those terrible acts.

Not only is the world an increasingly interconnected place; there are fewer and fewer places that are unaffected by this interconnectedness. There is little or no opportunity

---

[4] Roland Robertson, quoted in Malcolm Waters, *Globalization* (London: Routledge, 2001[2]), p. 4.

for Thoreau-like escapes into the wilderness. From electronic crofts in the Scottish Highlands to Amazon tribes using IT to market their craft products, you can run, but you can't hide.

Increased interconnectedness is taken to be the defining characteristic of globalization in *Global Transformations* by David Held et al.[5] The authors write of globalization as:

- A stretching of social, political and economic activities across frontiers, creating the possibility of action at a distance.
- An intensification of interconnectedness, that is, not random or occasional but regular.
- A speeding up of global interactions, so that people, ideas, capital and products now travel faster than before.
- The increasing impact of distant events, so that local events can have global consequences.

The outcome is a reversal of the adage to 'think global and act local' – now you can 'act local' and watch the global outcomes.

As we have seen, the FIFA World Cup of 2002 showed us this interconnectedness in action. Live sport beamed from Japan was watched in the Soweto slums; Senegalese supporters cheered their team in France. In the article from *The Observer* quoted at the start of this chapter an Italian journalist describes what it is like to live in three time zones: 'Japan time for football, Italy time for deadlines, New York time where I think I live'.

One world: increasing global consciousness

Looking out to a far horizon can be an aesthetically pleasing experience. I like to stand on a seashore, looking out to the

[5] David Held, Anthony McGrew, David Goldblatt and Jonathan Perraton, *Global Transformations* (Cambridge: Polity, 1999).

horizon, trying to grasp the sense of space and size that comes with such a perspective. Most of the time, however, my horizons are much more restricted – the horizon of my computer screen, the horizon of the road ahead as I drive, the horizon of the trees on the hills outside my town. For most people, horizons are fairly local, provided by friends and family, by home and work, and so on. But increasingly we have the experience, relatively new in human existence, of seeing the whole world as the horizon for our activities. Corporations do not produce products for local or national markets only – they produce for global markets. The Volks-wagen was produced for Hitler's Germany, and Henry Ford did the same for America with his Model T. Now the Ford Motor Company produces the Mondeo, marketed consciously as a 'world car'. Companies and individuals that excel in a given field are referred to as 'world class'.

Returning again to the example of football to illustrate this, FIFA have a global horizon. They have developed a strategy to expand soccer into a truly global sport. Prior to 1994, countries in Latin America and Europe, the game's traditional heartlands, alternated the hosting of the World Cup. Starting with USA 1994 and more recently with Korea/Japan 2002, and by expanding the number of teams present at the World Cup finals from twenty-four to thirty-two, FIFA has provided the opportunity for each continent to host the event and to have its representatives at the finals. FIFA President Sepp Blatter has promised South Africa the right to host the 2010 event, although whether it will actually do so is another question.

The environment: one interconnected world

Environmental issues are a good example of both increasing global interconnectedness and consciousness. We can see how actions in one part of the world have an effect on other parts of the world. Acid rain caused by UK factory emissions denudes Scandinavian pine forests. CFC emissions from refrigerators around the world cause a hole in the ozone layer above Antarctica. Greenhouse gas emissions lead to global warming and sea level rises that threaten Bangladesh with catastrophic flooding and the Maldive Islands with submersion. And we think of the world as a whole, as a single place, when trying to find global solutions, like at the Rio Earth Summit 1992, the 1997 Kyoto Protocol on greenhouse gas emissions and the Rio+10 Earth Summit in Johannesburg in 2002.

A new world (dis)order?

So where has this sense of a single, interconnected world come from? Is it that new, and why has it grabbed our attention at this time?

Estimates of when globalization started vary. Some suggest it has been developing since the dawn of history, as human societies first learned to trade and exchange both goods and ideas. Others argue that it is closely tied to the emergence of capitalism and the modern era. A further contention is that it is much more recent than that; that globalization is a characteristic of a post-industrial era, a phenomenon of disorganized and highly mobile capital. But whichever may be the case, all arguments accept that there has been a sudden recent acceleration in globalization in recent years.

Why the acceleration? Probably because of a variety of factors. Technological developments have created the opportunity. Travel is not quite instantaneous yet, but I can be anywhere in the world within twenty-four hours of writing these words. The words themselves can be anywhere in the world in seconds, thanks to e-mail and the web.

Economic factors have taken advantage of the possibilities provided by technology. Corporations have expanded into new and emerging markets and have shifted production around the world, in the cause of increased profits and a higher share price. Politically, the collapse of communism in Eastern Europe and the Soviet Union in the late 1980s and early 1990s signalled the end of the bipolar worldview created by the cold war and allowed the emerging multi-directional 'new world order' to become more visible. Some have suggested that we have moved from the Berlin Wall to a no-walls world, although I'm not sure it is as simple as that. Overall, we can say that there is no one single driver of global-ization. It is rather the outcome of a combination of factors, working together to produce this new sense of global inter-connectedness.

Some would dispute whether it is that new. The so-called 'world' religions of Christianity, Islam, Hinduism and Buddhism linked together major regions of the world in the early Middle Ages and before, creating civilizations far larger than most of today's nation states. The European empires of the 'high' colonial period of 1880–1920 oversaw a massive amount of global trade that declined considerably during the first half of the twentieth century, the era of Depression and protectionism. But medieval civilizations like Christendom knew very little of what was going on else-where in the world and the nineteenth-century colonial empires were controlled and dominated by European nation states. We need to draw a distinction between 'internation-alization', which includes mechanisms to facilitate commu-nication and co-operation between nation states (which remain dominant), and 'globalization', wherein the nation states are but one group of 'players' in the world, alongside transnational corporations, financial capital markets, free-trade areas and agreements, and transnational political entities like the United Nations and the European Union.

And if there are debates about where and how globalization started, then passions really begin to rise when the discussion moves on to what it means, and whether it is a good or bad thing.

The rising tide ... that lifts all boats

There are those who advocate globalization as a (largely) unmitigated good. They tend to define globalization in economic terms and look at the expansion of global trade, the decline in protectionism and the emergence of new markets as something that will improve not just those regions currently best placed to take advantage of the new opportunities. Eventually, all parts of the world will take a share of the increased prosperity that flows along every tributary of the new interconnected world. Closely linked to this is the decline of the power of the nation state, being replaced by 'region states'[6] such as Seattle–Vancouver, Barcelona–Catalonia, northern Italy, London–South East England and Hong Kong, Singapore and their immediate hinterlands. This new economic order is based on free-market capitalism and Western liberal democratic values, which 'defeated' socialism and communism and which are not threatened by viable alternatives.[7] Organizations such as the World Trade Organization have been developed to 'police' this new situation and to penalize nation states that refuse to play by its rules (trade disputes between the USA and the European Union are often referred to it, just as the EU now plays a role in arbitration in similar disagreements among its own member countries).

[6] Kenichi Ohmae, 'The Rise of the Region State', *Foreign Affairs* 72/2 (1993).

[7] Francis Fukuyama, 'The End of History?', *The National Interest* 16 (Summer 1989).

Not everyone is convinced that such deregulation, coupled with faith in the power of the market, will benefit all. Will the rising tide really raise all boats, or just the yachts and ocean-going motor-cruisers, leaving the junks, sampans and outrigger canoes behind to be swamped and flooded? Mass protests spilled over into riots at the World Trade Organization meetings in Seattle in 1999 and the G8 summit in Genoa in 2001,[8] giving a vivid illustration of the anger and lack of trust felt by many towards the unaccountable transnational corporations and wider economic forces that shape the future of so many communities without any opportunity for comeback. The so-called 'anti-globalization' movement (although it is probably fairer to say that many within the movement are against *economic* globalization, or simply concerned that it is not as equitable in sharing its largesse as some would hope) pushed the 'pro-globalizers' (free-marketeers, transnational corporations and the rest) on to the back foot for a while, but there are signs of something of a counter-offensive from the latter, with the argument that economic globalization along the lines described above is still the *best hope* for the world's poor and that they must be helped to take advantage of it.[9]

The UK government's Department for International Development takes this approach, recognizing that opposing globalization is probably now akin to opposing the sun rising, and, just as skin cancer can be prevented by the application of sun block, so globalization can be made to work *for* the world's poor, not against them.

---

[8] There were the same number of protestors (about 250,000) at the EU meetings in Barcelona in March 2002 and in Seville in June 2002 as at Genoa, even though this didn't erupt into the same kind of violence nor did it attract as much media attention.

[9] Charles Leadbeater, *Up the Down Escalator* (London: Viking, 2002).

Big Macs for all

Whenever I travel around the world (which is not as exciting as it sounds – airports are just big bus stations) I always take the opportunity to visit a McDonald's in the country that I am visiting – just once, and just because I can. It's always nice to eat British food when away from home! I'm always intrigued to see just how familiar the environment of a McDonald's restaurant is. The set menus 1–3 are always Big Mac, McChicken Sandwich and Quarterpounder meals. I can always get a vanilla shake. There are usually some intriguing local variations, such as the McBurrito and armed guards in Mexico or beer in France, but on the whole the environment is familiar (and also air-conditioned, a welcome relief in a hot and humid climate).

This global spread of McDonald's, with its standardized food and restaurant design, is another facet of globalization that arouses considerable angst. French farmer Jose Bové became a pin-up of the 'anti-globalization' movement when he trashed a local McDonald's restaurant with his tractor. Other French farmers have tipped trailer-loads of French apples outside McDonald's restaurants and even overturned the sacred statues of Ronald McDonald in similar protests against the perceived onslaught against French culture and food.

McDonald's are not alone in this now-global ubiquity. Nike, Levi, Coca-Cola, Starbucks, Gap, MTV, Marlboro, Blockbuster and so on all represent the emergence of the global superbrand. The high streets of every town begin to look the same. Terms like 'Coca-Colonization' and 'global consumer culture' are coined to imply that Western (usually American) consumer culture has been exported via the mass media to all parts of the globe. We should note that the phrase 'consumer culture' means more than just consumption. Items consumed, especially branded items, take on a symbolic value, so that the consumer asks not 'Does this brand represent good quality?' but 'What does this brand say about me?' Consumption becomes the main source of identity. Wearing Western brands becomes a simulated way of participating in the Western lifestyle and having a share of Western affluence. It becomes a way of expressing aspirations and even a person's sense of self.

McDonald's represents a good example of the contemporary homogenization of culture and its associated reduction of choice and local variation, according to George Ritzer.[10] 'McDonaldization' is a process by which consumer choice is rationalized and predetermined according to the principles of the fast food industry. The result – we can only have the products, and the cultural options, chosen on our behalf and offered to us by a decreasing number of global corporations. And these options are closely associated with and determined by the West, so that globalization becomes simply a euphemism for continued Western dominance of the world. Empire lives on after all, in Nike trainers and Gap khakis, smoking a Marlboro Light.

Ritzer suggests that the four characteristics of McDonaldization are:

- Efficiency – the time and effort expended to satisfy a want is reduced to as small a time as possible (it's shocking, I know, but sometimes you have to wait two to three minutes if there are no burgers ready at McDonald's!). McDonald's helps to fulfil this by keeping their menu as limited as possible.
- Calculability – value is determined by money, time and effort, not by less tangible notions such as quality (Burger King's burgers are usually regarded as being of a higher

---

[10] George Ritzer, *The McDonaldization of Society* (Thousand Oaks, California: Pine Forge Press, 1993).

standard than McDonald's, but Burger King lags behind in popularity).

- Predictability – products are standardized. A Big Mac in London tastes the same as it does in Paris, Sao Paulo and Kuala Lumpur (apparently, this is a selling point). A familiar product fosters security in the mind of the consumer.
- Control – limited and fixed menus, uncomfortable fixed seating, queue controls, standardized production systems and the like.

These principles underlie the success of the McDonald's brand and are evident in other fast food brands, but also beyond. Wal-Mart sells the same global brands in its stores in Berlin, Mexico City and Houston;[11] Gap's range of clothing is surprisingly limited; politicians carry pagers to ensure they are kept 'on message'; people who take a year out from their careers to go backpacking are seen as non-conforming troublemakers rather than useful individuals who will think differently and challenge the dominant consensus (or maybe it's because of the latter that they are seen as a problem).

Global economic systems that exploit the poor and benefit the rich. Limited cultural options that create a bland uniform world in the image of the West. No wonder globalization draws such ire.

But is that all there is to it?

New walls in a 'no-walls' world

I mentioned above that globalization has been seen as creating a 'no-walls' world. But we can see new walls being erected around the world, sometimes in direct response to

---

[11] *Newsweek*, 20 May 2002, p. 46.

the processes described above. Hirst and Thompson[12] argue that, in economic terms, globalization is a myth. International economic activity has not displaced the power of nation states. Instead, nation states are the primary drivers of this activity (hence, for example, the importance of the G8 industrialized countries).

In an article entitled 'Jihad vs McWorld',[13] Benjamin Barber outlined a similar trend in socio-cultural terms, contrasting the 'commercially homogenous global network' of McWorld with 'a threatened Lebanonization of national states in which culture is pitted against culture, people against people, tribe against tribe'. Barber called this latter sectarianism 'Jihad', and sees it as a reaction, an escape from McWorld's 'dully insistent imperatives'. In 'Jihad', the emphasis is on locality, community, culture and identity over against uniformity and economic efficiency. But while Barber believed that globalization would eventually defeat the retribalization of Jihad ('Jihad may be a last deep sigh before the eternal yawn of McWorld'), others are not so sure.

The article 'The Coming Anarchy'[14] by Robert Kaplan presents a frightening vision of a world torn by ethnic conflicts, ungovernable and subject to criminal anarchy. But his scenario presents ethnicity simply as a source of

---

[12] P. Hirst and G. Thompson, *Globalization in Question: The International Economy and the Possibilities of Governance* (Cambridge: Polity Press, 1996).

[13] Benjamin Barber, 'Jihad vs McWorld', *The Atlantic Monthly* (March 1992), reproduced in P. O'Meara, H. Mehlinger and M. Krain (eds), *Globalization and the Challenges of a New Century: A Reader* (Bloomington, Indiana: Indiana University Press, 2000).

[14] Robert Kaplan, 'The Coming Anarchy', *The Atlantic Monthly* (February 1994), reproduced in O'Meara et al, *Globalization and the Challenges of a New Century*.

hatred and exclusion rather than identity and meaning, and ignores the ability of diverse peoples to co-exist.

A more influential essay entitled 'The Clash of Civilisations'[15] by Harvard academic Samuel Huntington has benefited from a rekindling of interest in its basic thesis, following the World Trade Center atrocities of 11 September 2001. Huntington suggests that in future 'the clash of civilisations will dominate global politics'. Civilizations are cultural entities, including a large number of peoples and often a large number of countries. He suggests that there are eight main civilizations: Western, Slavic–Orthodox, Islamic, Hindu, Confucian, Japanese, Latin American and African. There are a number of reasons why civilizations clash, and especially so at this time:

- They are founded on basic differences of history, language, culture, tradition and, most important of all, religion.
- The world is becoming a smaller place. Because of the increased interconnectedness characteristic of globalization, interactions between different civilizations are increasing, leading to greater awareness of similarities and differences.
- The economic and social changes identified earlier in this chapter are weakening people's sense of identity, especially where this is tied to nationality. Religion provides not only a basis for civilization but also for identity.
- The West is at the height of its power, leading to a desire on the part of others for alternative sources of identity and power as a means of resisting its domination.
- Cultural characteristics do not change as easily as economic or political arrangements. Religion discriminates between people even more sharply than ethnicity.

---

[15] Samuel P. Huntington, 'The Clash of Civilisations?', *Foreign Affairs* 72/3 (1993).

As Huntington notes, it is possible to be half-French and half-Arab, but it is difficult to be half-Catholic and half-Muslim.
- Economic regionalization is increasing, and these arrangements are most successful when based on common civilizational codes, as in the European Union, the Chinese countries and diaspora of South-East Asia, and the North American Free Trade Area (whose success will depend, suggests Huntington, upon Mexico's ability to separate itself from the rest of Latin America and align itself more closely with the USA and Canada).

For these reasons, civilizational identities are strengthening, and clashes between civilizations are becoming more common.

While somewhat prescient in identifying Islam as providing a significant confrontation with the West, Huntington also missed the mark occasionally, suggesting that underlying differences between China and the USA could develop into a 'new cold war'. He did, however, also suggest that the main contour of civilizational conflict in the twenty-first century would be 'the West vs the Rest', wherein the 'Rest' either attempt to join the West and accepts its values and institutions, or attempt to balance the West by developing their own economic, military and cultural power bases – that is, modernizing without Westernizing. It is this latter approach that he thinks most likely, developing from a link between Confucian (Chinese) and Islamic civilizations.

All these observations provide us with a useful counterpoint to the assumption that globalization leads inexorably to Western economic and cultural hegemony. Through precisely the same mechanism – increasing global interconnectedness – Huntington suggests that both this and the opposite will occur, that is, increased economic and cultural resistance to Western domination.

Shuffling the deck

Western economic and cultural dominance are undeniable realities in the world today. The 'clash of civilizations' thesis and the superb expression 'Jihad vs McWorld' remind us that other forces are also in play at the same time. Western hegemony is being resisted. But are we being pushed into a false antithesis, forced to decide which will ultimately 'win': the forces of fragmentation or the forces of uniformity?

Globalization, defined earlier as increasing global inter-connectedness, is changing the economic, political and socio-cultural contours of modern societies. There is no longer an easy and clear distinction between what is local and what is international, or what is 'over there' and what is 'over here', since what happens 'over there' affects and influences 'over here', and vice versa. And we are less and less sure where 'here' ends and 'there' begins. Globalization represents neither the incorporation of more and more societies into a single homogenized global culture nor a fragmentation and hardening of local identities. Instead, it is about the increase in options in every locality and the power available to every locality to affect other localities elsewhere. Since this is not available to all equally, it creates new patterns of power and powerlessness, in which some in each country or region become more enmeshed in a global network, whereas others in the same country or region are increasingly marginalized.

You can run, but you can't hide

In this sense, then, globalization is about change. It is changing the way that people see themselves, so that they no longer define themselves only in relation to other nearby local realities, but also in relation to global realities and other localities on the other side of the world. Previously homogeneous cultural niches, hitherto able to exist purely on their own terms, are forced to think of themselves in relation to other cultures and outlooks from the world 'outside'. The deck of cards of the world's cultures is being shuffled and made ready for a new deal.

Returning (yes, again) to our football theme, the 2002 FIFA World Cup provided an example of this in relation to Japan. A number of eminent Japanese commentators saw in football an example of the kind of society that Japan needs to become – creative and imaginative, diverse and open to the outside world, rather than based on traditional Confucian values of unity and loyalty, and closed, to the point of xenophobia, to the outside world. Football offers a model blend of the old ethic of team solidarity with the new spirit of individual flair.[16] The image of hard-working conformist Japanese company-men was undermined by pictures of 2,000 young Japanese football fans hurling themselves into Osaka's Dotonbori canal (and shouting abuse at police who tried to stop them) in celebration of Japan topping a group that included Belgium and the old enemy, Russia. These celebrations were not, however, a rejection of their Japaneseness – rather, it represented a show of patriotism unseen since the Second World War, untainted by past militaristic associations. And nationalistic politicians proved unable to exploit the mood to their own ends. Tokyo governor Shintaro Ishihara called Phillippe Troussier, the French manager of the Japan squad, a 'second-rate bully' who represented the worst characteristics of white people, whereas most of Japan's young supporters admired him and chanted for 'Troussier

---

[16] < www.guardian.co.uk/Archive/Article/0,4273,4454789,00. html >.

Nippon', demanding a country based on merit rather than seniority, part of a global array of cultures rather than an insular nationalism.[17]

Saudi Arabia provides another example. For a long time a closed kingdom and renowned for its secrecy and resistance to un-Islamic external influence, it now represents a remarkable blend of modernity and the past, like 'Dallas policed by the Taliban'. The religious leaders in the town of Buraydah (whose residents are known as *mutawwa*, which means 'deeply devout Muslims' or 'fanatics', depending on your point of view) claim that 'This is the centre of Saudi Arabia. It is pure here. There is no mixing with other cultures.' They say, 'We allow all sorts of winds to come to us, but we don't let them blow us into the air. Mixing is one reason why people stray from righteousness.' Yet modern economic and cultural influences cannot be escaped in Saudi Arabia and mixing cannot be denied. Sony advertisements are placed on enormous hoardings built above mosques, women shop at Harvey Nichols in a Norman Foster building while fully shrouded, and McDonald's restaurants close their doors five times a day for prayer. Political debate has centred on the revelation that fifteen of the nineteen World Trade Center hijackers were Saudis, as is/was Osama Bin Laden himself. Saudi Arabia's fifty-year economic and military love affair with the West is coming under considerable internal pressure, with the USA now viewed as the 'first enemy of the Muslims' for its actions in relation to Israel and the Palestinians.[18]

---

[17] But even change has its limits. After stripping, diving and abusing the police, a crowd of Japanese football fans on their way home in Osaka waited patiently at a pedestrian crossing, even though there were no cars on the street. See < www.observer.co.uk/Print/0,3858,4434666,00.html >.

[18] < www.guardian.co.uk/g2/story/0,3604,747596,00.html >.

You're not from round here, are you?

The above cases are examples of a phenomenon known as *glocalization*. This term describes the way in which ideas and structures that circulate globally are adapted and changed by local realities. So while Wal-Mart sells Heinz and Del Monte products in its stores worldwide, it also pays close attention to local tastes. The Wal-Mart store in Shenzen, China, for example, sells chicken feet, Ma-Ling brand stewed pork ribs and Gulong brand pickled lettuce. About 85 per cent of the products come from 14,000 Chinese suppliers.[19]

McDonald's, that supposed pioneer of homogenized consumption, shows similar approaches to its local marketing. One finds numerous examples of adaptation to local tastes, such as the McBurrito in Mexico, McLlahua sauce in Bolivia (a local chilli sauce found on every meal table), beer on sale in French McDonald's restaurants and the Maharaja Mac in India (a mutton version of the Big Mac for a country where beef or pork consumption is risky to say the least). McDonald's recognizes that it is viewed by many as an example of American cultural and economic imperialism and asserts in response that it is instead a confederation of locally owned companies. It even ran adverts in France that poked fun at Americans and their food choices and which emphasized that its food was made in France, by French suppliers, using French products.[20] Even when the American identity of McDonald's is undeniable, it produces reactions that reinforce local identities. When McDonald's first entered the Philippines, Filipino hamburger chains responded by marketing their products on the basis of local taste (whereas they had previously promoted them on the basis of their Americanness).[21]

---

[19] *Newsweek*, 20 May 2002, p. 46.
[20] *New York Times*, 14 October 2001.
[21] Waters, *Globalization*, p. 226.

Now, global corporations like Wal-Mart and McDonald's don't adapt to local preferences because of a philosophical commitment to global diversity. They do so because they have discovered that local tastes are not easily changed or homogenized, but instead show considerable resilience in the face of 'global' flows of ideas and products. So it is possible to conclude that 'neither global processes nor modernisation are expressions of a westernisation that removes cultural differences ... localisation is an essential feature of global processes and modernisation' and that what we see are 'multiple manifestations of global forces operating in local worlds'.[22]

Baltis and Bollywood, Pokémon and Panasonic, feng shui and Falun Gong

As well as localizing adaptations, the idea that we are seeing the emergence of a bland, uniform commercial culture based on Western ideas is further undermined by the observation that other cultures are also using the processes of globalization to expand their reach. Non-Westernization is as much a feature of globalization as Westernization is.

So the most popular meal ordered in restaurants in the UK is the chicken tikka masala. The popularity of Indian food in the UK is shown by the existence of the 'Curry Mile' in Manchester and similar large groups of restaurants in cities around the UK. The Chinese takeaway is ubiquitous. And this movement and adaptation of food styles is not new. Consider that symbol of quintessential Englishness, the cup of tea. Tea is, of course, not grown in Britain, but

[22] Both quotations taken from Sverker Finnström, 'Postcoloniality and the Postcolony: Theories of the Global and the Local', Working Paper on Anthropology #7, University of Uppsala, Sweden (1997). Available at < 65.107.211.206/post/poldiscourse/finnstrom/finnstrom2.html >.

comes from China and India (where the British began farming it in 1835 to break the Chinese monopoly, so it's not that Indian either). Maybe in future a curry will be called an 'English', not an 'Indian'?

The Indian film industry, 'Bollywood', is not only bigger than Hollywood: it has plans for global expansion, as shown by the success of recent films like *Monsoon Wedding* and the Oscar-nominated *Lagaan*. Ang Lee's film *Crouching Tiger, Hidden Dragon* was a massive international hit, despite being a Chinese-language film with subtitles. Chinese cultural influence on the West can be seen in the popularity of feng shui[23] in interior and garden design and the interest shown in the persecuted Falun Gong religious movement. Even Hollywood itself, the ultimate visual purveyor of the American Dream, shows signs of sharing in this reshuffle of cultural influence, as some of its biggest studios are now foreign-owned, such as Sony (Japanese) and Vivendi Universal (French).

Pokémon, a cartoon whose rise to global domination of children's imaginations in 1999–2001 was spearheaded by a yellow, electric-shock-inducing mouse called Pikachu, is Japanese in style and origin from start to finish. Movies, computer games, trading cards and figurines tumbled over one another in a marketing blitzkrieg that swept children's allowances and parents' credit cards before it. Japanese goods also dominate the home entertainment market, and Japanese cars are produced and bought worldwide.

No place like home

So globalization is not producing a homogenized McWorld made in the image of the West. Jihad and McWorld are not

---

[23] There is no truth in the claim that feng shui is Chinese for 'tidy your room'!

a contradiction. Instead they are two sides of the same coin. Local variants based on tradition are produced as a reaction to outside influences. But local variants also develop through the flexibility of glocalization. These processes of localization are not simply coping reactions, but a feature of globalization itself. McDonaldization may be one aspect of globalization, but it is not the only or dominant feature. After all, 'An enormous range of individualised, unpredictable, inefficient and irrational products can be inspected simply by surfing the Internet.'[24] Production and consumption are being diversified, not restricted, as we will see in the next chapter. If we compare high street shops, food choices, variety in clothing styles, car design, or any other consumption pattern you care to name, we can see that the trend is towards more choice, not less. What is available in one locality becomes, because of globalization, available in all localities. In any given locality, the range of consumption choices and of cultural opportunities is increased. Local homogeneity is not replaced by global homogeneity but by global and local diversity.

Francis Fukuyama's famous essay 'The End of History?'[25] argued that Western liberal democracy has 'won' because of the absence of alternatives since the demise of communism. Perhaps we would be more accurate to argue that we are now seeing 'The End of Geography'. Our sense of space is compressed because of the speed of communication enabled by information technology and because we are increasingly used to seeing the world as a whole. But more than this, we can now no longer equate certain cultures with certain places. Huge migratory flows have created large and diverse population variations across the world. The flow of ideas, images and products has introduced

---

[24] Waters, *Globalization*, p. 229.
[25] Fukuyama, 'The End of History?'.

possibilities for new identity options to dominant and marginalized cultures alike. Cultures are no longer defined by place but are deterritorialized. Globalization is leading to 'one world' not because it homogenizes but because the effects of geography and of distance are decreasing. We will explore the implications of this for identity and culture in a later chapter. At present, we can note that 'home' is an increasingly alien concept in the fluid, mobile, pluralizing world of globalization.[26]

The observant reader will have noticed that I have only dealt here with globalization in relation to culture and not at all with the question of whether globalization is an extension of Western economic dominance, or if it instead constitutes the 'best hope' for poor nations too. This is a large and complex topic that is outside my expertise and beyond the scope of this book. It has been expertly addressed elsewhere by others.[27]

In the next chapter, we explode another myth: 'one size fits all'.

---

[26] An issue explored in detail by Zygmunt Bauman in *Globalization: The Human Consequences* (Cambridge: Polity Press, 1998).

[27] See, for example, Bob Goudzwaard, *Globalization and the Kingdom of God* (Grand Rapids, Michigan: Baker, 2001); Noreena Hertz, *The Silent Takeover* (London: Heinemann, 2001); Peter Heslam, *Globalization: Unravelling the New Capitalism* (Cambridge: Grove, 2002); Naomi Klein, *No Logo* (London: HarperCollins, 2000); Tom Sine, *Mustard Seed Versus McWorld: Reinventing Christian Life and Mission for the New Millennium* (Crowborough: Monarch, 1999).

Chapter 2

One Size Fits All, or Made To Measure?

Postmodernity, choice and its limits

In the book *Life after God* by Douglas Coupland, the narrator recounts his driving across the Mojave Desert in the south-western USA, thinking about his personal emotional state, his beliefs and the nature of belief. He finds himself listening to Christian radio stations.

> The radio stations all seemed to be talking about Jesus non-stop, and it seemed to be this crazy orgy of projection, with everyone projecting onto Jesus the antidotes to the things that had gone wrong in their own lives. He is Love. He is Forgiveness. He is Compassion. He is a Wise Career Decision. He is a Child Who Loves Me.
>
> And yet I had to ask myself over and over what it was that these radio people were seeing in the face of Jesus. They sounded like their lives had once been so messed up and lost as they spoke; at least they were no longer so lost any more – like AA people. So I figured that was a good thing.[1]

These musings illustrate well a way of thinking about faith and about life that can be described as 'postmodern': postmoderns are neither antagonistic towards nor strongly

[1] Douglas Coupland, *Life after God* (London: Simon & Schuster, 1994), pp. 183–4.

interested in a belief system different from their own; they are simply glad that the belief system seems to 'work' for other people.

Not more guff about postmodernity!

It is hardly new and cutting edge to write about post-modernity and its implications for the church. Yet we have tended to concentrate on its manifestations in the areas of belief rather than practice (much as I have done by selecting the above quotation). It is somewhat commonplace now to talk about 'postmodern relativism' (as though relativism is a recent invention and not one of the major contributions of modernity – in fact, postmodernity can be seen as the use of the weapons of modernity, including relativism, on modernity itself).

At this point I would like to make an artificial (but I believe helpful) distinction between postmodern*ism* and postmodern*ity*. The former refers to the ideas and philo-sophical thinking, usually French, which define this out-look. The latter refers more to the conditions, the ways of behaving, which can be characterized as postmodern with-out necessarily being underpinned by or even aware of the ideas of postmodernism.

That said, let's begin by looking at some of the main aspects of postmodern thought. We'll come back to postmodernity later. To do so, we need to go back even further, beginning with the ideas usually described as characteristic of modernity.

Modernity can be rooted in the ideas which emerged following the devastating European religious wars of the early seventeenth century, such as the Thirty Years War (1618–1648), when Protestant and Catholic countries and kingdoms in Europe fought, ravaged and destroyed one another in the name of Jesus Christ, of the church and of truth. Dismayed by these atrocious events, people began to search for an approach to truth that could transcend such sectarian divisions. At the heart of this response, human reason was elevated above divine revelation as the best guide to the ordering of society and to the discovery of truth (after all, over a hundred years of everything from bickering to genocide had marked the immediately preceding era, much of which was shaped by the fault lines created and reflected in the Reformation).

Hallmarks of modern thought include:

- Humanism – the human being is the source of meaning and value. 'Man is the Measure of All Things'.[2]
- Rationalism – there is a natural human faculty of reason, moving from universal principles to particular applications.
- Secular moralism – human reason alone can allow moral action and moral society, if we can be freed from the superstition and prejudice of religious dogmatism.
- Progress – human history is progressive: moderns are more humane and moral, because of the public use of reason, than people of previous ages.

If you were unable to read the above list without allowing yourself a wry smile or a mental 'Yeah, right!' then you are probably more postmodern than you thought. The myth of objective truth that can be obtained by anyone and everyone using human reason alone is a seductive one, but one which has proved both impossible to attain and which has caused more human suffering and misery than the religious differences it was supposed to overcome.[3]

---

[2] Protagoras, *c*.490–*c*.420 BC.

[3] We should not confuse 'objective truth open to all' with the gospel – the latter isn't attained or understood by unaided human reason, but through a work of the Holy Spirit.

The problem with human reason is that it doesn't bring about the discovery of the universally applicable objective truths that it aspires to. The personal and subjective experiences and prejudices of human beings always seem to get in the way. More than this, we cannot dissociate any claims of absolute, universally applicable truth from the person or persons making the claim. We have to ask ourselves the question 'What do they get out of this?'

The modern assumption of universal truth, open and applicable to all, is given the name 'metanarrative', and it was Jean-François Lyotard who coined the now-classic definition of postmodernism as 'incredulity towards metanarratives', that is, an unwillingness to believe that any metanarrative could be valid and true for all. He pointed out that historical events such as Auschwitz have opened up a fissure in the great discourses of modernity (e.g. of reason and progress). All metanarratives include a 'vanguard' (usually its advocates and those for whom it is of primary benefit), although there is an expectation that eventually all of humanity will be included within it. When this doesn't happen (since there are always those who reject the metanarrative or who are excluded by it) the 'vanguard' faces the possibility of failure. This produces a type of grief or mourning for unanimity, and most commonly leads to an attempt to 'conquer' those who are different, who rejected or are rejected by the metanarrative. But this conquest is not exercized on behalf of all; now it is on behalf of 'us', and 'our' metanarrative.

Exposing the power play implicit in all claims to universal truth was also of concern to Michel Foucault. He suggested that we should ask 'Who says it has to be that, and not this?' He did not think of power as something used by the strong to dominate the weak, but rather saw it as simply a phenomenon of all human relationships.

Power is not something present at specific locations within (human) networks, but is instead always at issue in ongoing attempts to (re)produce effective social alignments or to avoid or erode their effects, often by producing various counteralignments.[4]

I think we too easily come to the conclusion that since the gospel of Jesus Christ includes some claim to universal applicability it too is therefore a metanarrative and so is something that is being attacked by postmodernist thought. But even a superficial reading of the life and teaching of Jesus Christ should allow us to see that, while some followed him, others rejected him. In fact, those who might have been expected to accept him and his teachings were those most likely to do the opposite (John 1:10–11), and there is a clear expectation in the New Testament that many will ultimately reject Jesus and his teaching (e.g. Matthew 25:31–46; Revelation 20:11–15). Nowhere are we permitted to exercize the fantasy that eventually all will be convinced by the truth of the gospel and that we should therefore set out to 'help' or 'educate' people of their error.[5]

Postmodernist thought, at its heart, looks for the things that refuse assimilation, the 'remainder', the outsider, on the basis that 'difference produces identity' (if there is anything close to a sound bite summary of postmodern concerns, this is it). It is this openness to difference, indeed an affirmation of the importance of difference, that characterizes the postmodern agenda.

---

[4]   G. Gutting, *The Cambridge Companion to Foucault* (Cambridge: Cambridge University Press, 1994), pp. 109–10.

[5]   It is true that, from time to time, 'Christian' kings found it politically expedient to enforce allegiance to Christianity as the state religion, as, for example, did Charlemagne with the Saxons. However, I'm not sure we would consider him to be an example that we would wish to follow.

Any colour you want, as long as it's Pepper Red, Metropolis Blue, Neptune Green ...

Henry Ford, the American car maker and industrialist, is famously credited with saying of his famous Model T: 'You can have it any colour you want as long as it's black.' Standardized production techniques produced the first car-ownership boom in 1920s America, bringing car ownership within the reach of even those on modest incomes.

How far have we come from that situation?

An article written in *The Observer* newspaper of 4 April 1999 discussed the rise of an 'I-Society' in Britain, that is, a generation that has rejected the 'me' culture of the 1980s for one which values 'individuality, independence, identity and interactivity'. The issues of individuality and identity are at the core of questions in contemporary culture. The question of identity is reflected in a lot of current contemporary music. For example, Cerys Matthews of Catatonia sings of some day finding the 'one who lives inside my mind' in the song 'Dazed, Beautiful and Bruised'.

Of great importance in creating these issues is the shift to a post-industrial society. In the highly successful British film *The Full Monty* a change in lifestyle is forced upon the protagonists by the closure of the steelworks in which they had previously worked. Philosophers, theologians and preachers of all kinds need to be aware that people's beliefs and values are sometimes more shaped by their behaviour and lifestyles, rather than vice versa.

So how might we characterize post-industrial society? As the change from manufacturing industry to service sector jobs; the change from the factory gate to the shopping mall; the change from production line to workstations in cubicles; the change from machine tools to information technology; the change from terraced housing to executive homes.

Life is becoming more diverse, more fragmented, more individualistic (note the hilarity that attended the news that Hillary Clinton's fiftieth birthday party in 1997 was attended by her five hundred 'closest personal friends'), and so the outlook shaped by post-industrial society is one that focuses, as we noted above, on identity, on who we are.

In a consumer society our self-definition comes mainly from the products we buy and the brands we identify with (Pepsi or Coke, Gap or Levis?). As we noted earlier, the core question about brands now is not 'Is this a quality product?' but 'What does this brand say about me?' Since we are now looking for individuality, 'our' own unique identity, 'our' genetic blueprint, we don't want to look and be the same as everyone else. We want to be distinct, 'us'. This means that we live in a day not of mass-production but of mass-customization.

In Spring 2000, while doing research for an article, I visited the Ford UK web site, which showed that it then offered nine different cars for sale in the UK (Ka, Fiesta, Escort, Focus, Mondeo, Puma, Cougar, Galaxy, Explorer). Taking the Ford Focus alone, you could have had a choice of four body shapes (three-, four-, five-door saloon, plus estate), four levels of specification (CL, Zetec, LX, Ghia) and five different engines (1.4, 1.6, 1.8, 2.0, 1.8 tdi). You then had choice of eleven colours. So there were 880 different Ford Focus options, before even beginning to think about interior seat trim or optional extras. Now it's even better: at the *www.fordconnection.co.uk* web site you can design your preferred car online, including the trim, a variety of other specifications and all optional extras, which will then be built to order. It's great to play with – I've designed a number of cars I'd love to buy, only to fall at the final hurdle – the payment fence. Most car parts now being assembled on a Ford production line have the customer's name already attached to them.[6] It makes Dell's PCs-made-to-order approach sound slightly less impressive when you realize they're doing it for cars as well.

Adverts for the household paint Dulux show a woman stealing some lilac underwear from a neighbour's washing line, or cutting a patch from a yellow hooded top worn by a shaven-headed bodybuilder sat in front of her on a bus. In both adverts, we then cut to shots of the same woman just finishing some interior decorating, with the room painted in exactly the same colour as the stolen item. In other words, if you can't find the colour you like from the hundreds already on offer in your nearest DIY megastore, then they will mix up another, just for you.

The Nike iD service at the www.nike.com/europe web site allows you to customize a pair of football boots or running shoes. You choose from a variety of colours, select your shoe size or simply input the length of your foot in millimetres, and your name and number are added to the boot tongue and heel. The boots are then made to order and shipped directly to your home. Nike's great rival in the sports footwear stakes, Adidas, have gone even further than this. In 1986, rap pioneers Run-DMC sang about 'My Adidas' (which the shoe firm neatly exploited by giving the band free pairs of their sneakers to throw into the audience at their gigs, thereby reinforcing brand loyalty and its 'street-cool' image in one deft stroke). They have now taken the theme one step further, with the 'mi adidas' custom shoemaker. This includes a device to measure foot length and width and a running track that computes the amount and type of support needed. Outsole, design, size, colour and logo are then decided on and, $120 later, the perfect shoe arrives on your doormat.

---

[6] Michael Moynagh, *Changing World, Changing Church* (London: Monarch, 2001), p. 19.

The other rising star of the sports shoe world (or, more accurately, a comet returning to prominence) is Puma. Started by the brother of Adi Dassler (guess which company he founded?) its co-president Mark Parker recently commented:

> The future for us isn't going to be, hey, here's better shoes, better apparel, better product. It's going to be a lot more dimensionalised … Customisation and the personalisation of products and services are going to be a bigger and bigger part of our future.[7]

This mass-customization of society has moved beyond the products that we buy to the information and knowledge we receive. Talk of an 'information explosion' is common, through the development and expansion of satellite/cable/digital TV, the now-ubiquitous CD-ROMs and DVDs, and, of course, the Internet. In response to this, we see the development of tailored communications. 'Old' media, such as newspapers, and music producers are having to adapt to the demands of the consumers of 'new' media, such as the ability to interact with web sites and to personalize both the services and content received. Similar 'tailoring' can be seen in the propensity to talk of 'narrowcasting' rather than 'broadcasting'; in direct-marketers working with smaller and smaller segments of the population; and in the use of 'cookies', which allow web sites to identify return visitors, to retain their personal information for future use, and to offer services such as those provided by the www.amazon.co.uk web site, such as 'recommendations' (based on your previous buying patterns), and 'people who bought this book also bought …'[8]

---

[7] Geraldine Bedell, 'The Changing Face of the Brand', *The Observer* Review section, 19 January 2003, pp. 1–2.

[8] Many more examples of the above can be found in Gerard Kelly, *Get A Grip on the Future without Losing your Hold on the Past* (London: Monarch, 1999), pp. 59–92; Moynagh, *Changing World, Changing Church*, pp. 18–34; Richard

This is the key theme of much marketing in the West – whatever suits 'you'. Personal individuality, and customization to that individuality, is the order of the day.

Welcome to the pick 'n' mix counter

The above examples all provide us with an idea of what postmodern*ity* is all about: the expansion of choice and the tailoring of those choices to your own personal needs, wants and whims create an experienced world where postmodern ideas seem to make sense and so are more widely accepted. In short, they provide a 'plausibility structure' for those behaviours and associated ideas to thrive.

And globalization, by bringing ideas, values and belief systems from other places into our world, only serves to increase even further the number of options open to us.

The idea that human identity is not a given, but is something that we make, is termed 'constructivism'. All culture is learned – every human baby is born a 'clean slate'. But in most places, for most of human history, who that child grew up to be and what he or she grew up to believe was to a large extent determined by the context in which he or she lived. Culture gives a child the tools and the framework needed to develop his or her own identity (so constraining and limiting the options – you wouldn't expect a radical feminist identity to be constructed in a fundamentalist Christian or Muslim culture). It has, of course, always been possible to change one's identity to some degree (the Christian notion of conversion is based on just such a possibility), but it is probably fair to say that because of the twin

---

[8] (*continued*) Tiplady, 'Let X = X: Generation X and World Mission' in William D. Taylor (ed.), *The Iguassu Dialogue: Global Missiology for the 21ˢᵗ Century* (Grand Rapids, Michigan: Baker, 2000), pp. 463–75.

influences of globalization and postmodernity there are now more options available to more people than has been the normal experience of humanity throughout history.

> **The human being is the only animal that can say things like 'I'm going to move to San Diego, grow my hair, and lose 20 pounds.'**
>
> *Douglas Coupland in 'Close Personal Friend',*
> *a promotional film that accompanied the*
> *launch of his 1995 book* Microserfs.

So we face an array of 'off-the-peg' and 'bespoke' identities, each presenting itself to us as an option. The result? We try to wear several of these outfits at the same time, adopting a chameleon approach to life. We have no choice but to make a choice (or choices).

And this leads to another problem. For there you are presented with an array of choices. Many of those choices can be tailored to fit exactly who you are. But who is the 'you' that the products are being tailored to fit? In a developed consumer society, much of our source of identity comes from the brands we identify with. So now the brand is being tailored to fit the person who defines him or herself by what the brand 'says about him or her'. And so we disappear up our own ... created selves.

The inherent flaw in the notion of self-reinvention is illustrated by the differing approaches of two of Douglas Coupland's novels that deal with this subject. His 1995 novel *Microserfs*[9] focuses on a group of friends who work for Microsoft and who decide to escape the faceless conformity of working for a major corporation by pooling their skills and

---

[9] Douglas Coupland, *Microserfs* (London: Flamingo, 1995).

(limited) financial resources in order to start a small software company.[10] It is a hopeful story that embodies the optimistic wish to 'start again', and, despite setbacks and challenges, it ends on a positive note. Coupland's *Miss Wyoming*,[11] published in 2000, also deals with the topic of self-reinvention. One of the two main characters, Susan Colgate, is a former child TV star and winner of many teen pageants who takes the opportunity provided by being the only survivor in a plane crash to disappear and reinvent herself. She ultimately fails, and (somewhat cheesily) only finds happiness when she meets the other protagonist, John Johnson, a fading former action movie star who has also tried to disappear. Both find redemption in the other: someone who accepts the other for who they are, not who they try to become.

The emptiness of self-reinvention without any basis in reality and the loss of personal cohesion and a central anchor of identity is summed up in the pitiful figure who encountered Jesus in the region of the Gerasenes, across the Lake of Galilee. 'My name is Legion … for we are many' (Mark 5:9). As Richard Middleton and Brian Walsh comment: 'Controlled by many spirits, the man in the biblical story was tormented, homeless and in need of healing. So, it seems to us, is the contemporary postmodern psyche.'[12]

This emptiness is summed up in a term used by postmodern philosopher Jean Baudrillard: *simulacrum*. The

---

[10] By way of an aside, it's interesting to note that, had the novel been written four years later, the protagonists would have started a dot.com business. The characters in the novel use e-mail, but there's no mention of the Internet, which didn't exist in any meaningful way to most people when the novel was being written.

[11] Douglas Coupland, *Miss Wyoming* (London: Flamingo, 2000).

[12] J. Richard Middleton and Brian J. Walsh, *Truth is Stranger than it Used to Be: Biblical Faith in a Postmodern Age* (London: SPCK, 1997), p. 56.

first level of simulation is the *counterfeit*, which usually bears a very close resemblance to the original, and in fact claims to be the original. Moving to a second level, we come to the *production*, which is a copy of an original that makes no claim to be the original, but which bears some obvious relation to it. An example of this would be the reproductions of a Monet or a Mark Rothko painting sold to the (un)discerning masses in shops like Athena and IKEA. Finally, at the third level, we come to the *simulacrum* or the *hyperreal*, which can be summed up as 'a copy of something for which the original was simply a mould, or which never existed in the first place'. Andy Warhol's famous prints of Marilyn Monroe, Elvis Presley, or the Campbell's soup tins begin to edge towards this, since he did so many versions of them. Which was the original? Does it matter? A more contemporary example would be a copy of a file e-mailed to someone else – which is the original, and which is the copy? Both are exact duplicates of the other.

Baudrillard suggested that Disneyland is a perfect model of a *simulacrum*, for it is all a play of illusions. 'Main Street USA' in Disneyland (which I visited a few years ago) purports to resemble an archetypal American small-town main street, but it doesn't exist anywhere else. It is a copy of something that doesn't exist. Even more worrying, suggests Baudrillard, is that:

> Disneyland is presented as imaginary in order to make us believe that the rest is real, when in fact all of Los Angeles and the America surrounding it are no longer real, but of the order of hyperreal and of simulation.[13]

---

[13] Jean Baudrillard, 'Simulacra and Simulations' in Mark Poster (ed.), *Jean Baudrillard: Selected Writings* (Stanford: Stanford University Press, 1988). Available from < www.stanford.edu/dept/HPS/Baudrillard/Baudrillard_Simulacra.html >.

The 'disneyfication' of our cities is well underway. Public space is being increasingly colonized by private shopping malls that provide entertainment and a shopping 'experience', not just products for sale. And whereas traditional shopping streets are diverse and compete visually for our attention, retail establishments in the malls are uniform and complementary. And we are aware that they are not real; they too are *simulacra*, copies of a reality that doesn't exist:

> Like the pod-bred clones in the science fiction movies *Invasion of the Body Snatchers* they seem to be genuine, but something isn't quite right. What's missing is a sense of the serendipity, diversity and humanity of traditional street life.[14]

This hyperreality extends even as far as the local corner shop. Middleton and Walsh call the culture of late advanced modernity 'a Cool Whip society', since 'Cool Whip is hyperreal whipped cream, cheaper, more durable and far less calorific than the real thing. Cool Whip does not need whipping and is free of cholesterol.'[15] A similar example from the UK is Utterly Butterly, described on its web site as 'a buttery tasting spread, high in monosaturates and low in saturates', the ingredients of which are 'Vegetable Oil; Reconstituted Buttermilk (30%); Hydrogenated Vegetable Oil; Salt (1.7%); Emulsifiers – E471, Soya Lecithin; Lactic Acid; Flavouring; Colours – Annatto, Curcumin; Vitamins A & D',[16] as opposed to butter, which is made from ... well, milk, really.

---

[14] John Hannigan, 'Fantasy Cities', *New Internationalist* 308 (December 1998), p. 20.

[15] Middleton and Walsh, *Truth is Stranger than it Used to Be*, p. 38.

[16] < www.utterly-butterly.co.uk/prodinfo.html >.

So where has this taken us?

From postmodernism we learn the principle that identity is produced by difference. The trend towards mass-customization and personalized articles of clothing reinforces this highlighting of difference. The outcome is a strong and growing concern for individuality and the emergence of bewildering diversity. Increasing choice opens our eyes to the possibility of reinvention, though we have noted above some of the limits to the success of such attempts.

But before we dismiss the contemporary concern for personal reconstruction and its concomitant diversification of society, we should note that all human cultures are constructs, and as such are perfectly legitimate attempts to make sense of the cacophony of reality. The human propensity for culture making is part of our createdness, and it is this predisposition that we will consider in the next chapter.

Chapter 3

Cain and Babel

A theology of cultural diversity

Tunisia is famous for its Roman mosaics. It is also known for its linguistic mosaic. The landscape is extremely colourful. A significant number of language varieties coexist on Tunisian soil. There are national languages and foreign languages. The national languages consist mainly of Standard Arabic (the official language), a cluster of Arabic dialects, and the Berber language, which is also split into regional varieties. The foreign languages are French, Spanish and Italian, which were added under the Protectorate system exercised in Tunisia by France and Italy from 1881 to 1956. To add further complexities to the kaleidoscope of languages, English has of late made its entry on the linguistic stage as a Brobdingnag[1] in the land of Lilliputians.[2]

The above quotation summarizes the theme of the first two chapters of this book, namely that cultural diversity is normal experience in most, if not all, of today's world. Even

---

[1] The Brobdingnagians feature in part 2 of *Gulliver's Travels* and were as gigantic as the Lilliputians were tiny.

[2] Mongi Bahloul, 'English in Carthage, or The Tenth Crusade', a paper given at the PostColonialismS/PoliticalCorrectnesseS conference, Casablanca, Morocco, 12–14 April 2001, p. 2. Available at < www.victorianweb.org/post/poldiscourse/casa blanca/program.html >.

apparently monolithic cultures such as Saudi Arabia are experiencing a creeping permeation of influence from other places. Cultural crossroads like Tunisia reflect the same processes to a far greater degree. But how should we view this diversification? Is it something to be welcomed, or to be resisted? The normal human reaction to infiltration by outsiders is to resist it (as we can note from the reactions in Western Europe to migration from elsewhere). Is it possible to discern any divine purpose in the changes that we have been describing? Is it possible to argue, for example, as some have done (somewhat simplistically) that 'God is bringing the nations of the world to the West so that they may be more easily evangelized'? If that were really the case, I look forward to the day when the unevangelized of the world, including Western Europeans, continue their migration onwards to Latin America and Africa, since that is where much of the vibrancy and life in contemporary Christianity may be found.

It is very difficult to come to any definitive conclusions about where God might be 'at work' in the vicissitudes of human history. Any attempts to come up with answers are in danger of breaching the third commandment, which tells us not to 'misuse the name of the LORD your God' (Exodus 20:7).

> The problem seems to be that Christians tend to sacralize the sociological forces of history that are dominant at any particular time, regarding them as inexorable works of providence or even of redemption.[3]

As the late-eighteenth-century English vicar Melvill Horne observed, divine providence is 'a mysterious book, not

---

[3] David Bosch, *Transforming Mission* (Maryknoll, New York: Orbis, 1991), p. 429.

easily legible, and best understood when read backward',[4] that is, from the vantage point of history, although quite how distant a point is needed is shown by the (probably apocryphal) response of Chairman Mao when asked what he thought were the long-term implications of the French and American Revolutions – 'It's too early to tell.'

Another challenge facing us as we try to discern the work of God in the time in which we live is that the canonical examples that we are given, usually through the Old Testament prophets, serve to emphasize the point that the way God works in history is not necessarily the way that we might expect or like. Isaiah reassured Ahaz, king of Judah, when he was attacked by the allied forces of Pekah, king of Israel, and Rezin, king of Syria, with the promise that the terrible army of Assyria would come and defeat his enemies, even though the outcome would be the devastation of the country of Israel and the setting up of Assyrian idols in the Jerusalem Temple (Isaiah 7:1–25; 9:1–5; 2 Kings 16:5–18). And this was meant to be the work of God? Habakkuk had similar concerns when he complained about the endemic injustice in the nation of Judah, and received the response that the Babylonian army would be the divine agent of justice upon his people.

A further consideration is that, when we think about the unity/diversity spectrum, there are pros and cons to each extreme. Diversity may allow the free expression of difference, but it can also lead to fragmentation, division and isolation. An emphasis on unity may counteract these tendencies, but can also manifest itself through pressures towards conformity and the marginalization and exclusion of those who do not obey the rules. In terms of the triad of values of the French Revolution, fraternity does not sit

[4] Melvill Horne, *Letters on Missions, Addressed to the Protestant Ministers of the British Churches* (Bristol, 1794).

easily alongside liberty and equality. Walter Bagehot observed:

> You may talk of the tyranny of Nero; but the real tyranny is the tyranny of your next-door neighbour. What law is so cruel as the law of doing what he does? What yoke is so galling as the necessity of being like him? Public opinion is a permeating influence, and it exacts obedience to itself; it requires us to think other men's thoughts, to speak other men's words, to follow other men's habits.[5]

Having noted these various provisos, we can now move on to thinking about how to respond theologically to the realities of contemporary cultural diversification.

Thank God for Babel: developing a theology of cultural diversity

> Then God said, 'Let us make man in our image, in our likeness, and let them rule over the fish of the sea and the birds of the air, over the livestock, over all the earth, and over all the creatures that move along the ground.' So God created man in his own image, in the image of God he created him; male and female he created them. God blessed them and said to them, 'Be fruitful and increase in number; fill the earth and subdue it. Rule over the fish of the sea and the birds of the air and over every living creature that moves on the ground' (Genesis 1:26–28).

The above event takes place at the climax of the first story of creation, on the sixth day. Humanity is created in the divine

---

[5] Quoted by Robert Putnam, *Bowling Alone: The Collapse and Revival of American Community* (New York: Touchstone, 2001), pp. 351–2.

image and is awarded stewardship of the rest of the created order that preceded it.

But what does it mean to be created in God's image? It may mean, among other things, that we share some of the characteristics of God. Not the difficult ones like omnipresence (being everywhere at the same time) and omniscience (knowing everything), but perhaps aspects such as relationship and creativity. More significant, however, is the command to 'fill the earth and subdue it'. This is where the human capacity for constructing culture comes in. Cultures can be seen as attempts to bring order into human experience, to make sense of the cacophony of reality, to organize human life in such a way that society can function in relative harmony. Common beliefs and values and permitted and proscribed behaviours help us to live in elationship with one another: 'For individuals, national culture is a strong element of identity, providing a framework of assumptions within which others' reactions can be anticipated and judged.'[6]

And so the human capacity for culture making is fundamentally good, based as it is on the divine image in all people and in the command given by God to humanity to 'subdue' the earth.

Unfortunately, however, the Genesis story does not stop at the end of chapter 1 (if it had, we wouldn't have needed the rest of the Bible). The story of the origins of human sin and separation from God, recounted in Genesis 3–4, shows the consequences of our now-fallen state. Humanity's relationship with the very earth that we are meant to steward is corrupted, as are all human relationships. Ultimately, we are now compelled (like Cain, who murdered his brother Abel) to wander through the cosmos, looking for a home.

---

[6] Simon Caulkin, 'Mission Impossible', *The Observer* Business section, 25 July 1999.

But this does not mean that the human capacity for culture making has been destroyed in the process. Sin has not eradicated God's image in humanity; rather it has merely corrupted it. We catch an intriguing glimpse of early human cultural development in an obscure part of Genesis 4:

> Cain lay with his wife, and she became pregnant and gave birth to Enoch. Cain was then building a city, and he named it after his son Enoch ... Lamech [fifth in descent from Cain] married two women, one named Adah and the other Zillah. Adah gave birth to Jabal; he was the father of those who live in tents and raise livestock. His brother's name was Jubal; he was the father of all who play the harp and flute. Zillah also had a son, Tubal-Cain, who forged all kinds of tools out of bronze and iron (Genesis 4:17–22).

Encapsulated in this passage are recollections of changes in agricultural practice, from hunter-gatherer to nomadic pastoralist. Other forms of human social organization, this time urban, are also indicated. We see the emergence of the arts, specifically music, and also the development of early technology, such as metalworking, tools and musical instruments. What makes this passage all the more intriguing is that these cultural developments are the product of Cain, the über-sinner, and his descendants. The cultural mandate given at creation is not destroyed by sin, but simply twisted and corrupted. Both the divine image in humanity and human fallenness are reflected in human culture.

Human cultures are therefore a mix of good and bad, and, just as my own personal weaknesses are so often the flipside of my strengths, so it is with human cultures. Western individualism may lead to fragmentation and isolation, but it is also based on a very real sense of the value of each and every human person. We may look at more communitarian societies and envy their social cohesion without being aware of the very strong control exerted by some upon others (usually the strong upon the weak, men upon women, and so on), that is, what is called the 'dark side of social capital'.[7] It is not easy to separate out the good from the bad and to keep only the former. Jesus Christ told us as much:

> The kingdom of heaven is like a man who sowed good seed in his field. But while everyone was sleeping, his enemy came and sowed weeds among the wheat, and went away. When the wheat sprouted and formed ears, then the weeds also appeared. The owner's servants came to him and said 'Sir, didn't you sow good seed in your field? Where then did the weeds come from?' 'An enemy did this,' he replied. The servants asked him, 'Do you want us to go and pull them up?' 'No,' he answered, 'because while you are pulling the weeds, you may root up the wheat with them. Let them both grow until the harvest' (Matthew 13:24–30).

Jesus did state that a judgement upon the sinful elements of human culture would happen, but that this judgement would be eschatological, not in human history. And the reason he gave was that any attempt to root out that which is unwanted now could easily eradicate things that are worth keeping. This is part of what it means to live in a fallen and yet redeemed world – we have to accept the ambiguity inherent in all human cultures and live with it, however unwelcome that may be.

So diversity and unity both have advantages, but they also both have disadvantages. Either one of them is not inherently better than the other. The trends towards diversification we have identified so far in this book are not intrinsically better or worse than what has gone before. They are different, perhaps more complex, but not worse.

---

[7] Putnam, *Bowling Alone*, p. 350.

And they may even be better. To consider this, we turn to one of humanity's other early cultural enterprises, the building of the Tower of Babel.

Now the whole world had one language and a common speech. As men moved eastward, they found a plain called Shinar and settled there. They said to each other, 'Come, let's make bricks and bake them thoroughly.' They used brick instead of stone, and bitumen for mortar. Then they said, 'Come, let us build ourselves a city, with a tower that reaches to the heavens, so that we may make a name for ourselves and not be scattered over the face of the earth.' But the LORD came down to see the city and the tower that the men were building. The LORD said, 'If as one people speaking the same language they have begun to do this, then nothing they plan to do will be impossible for them. Come, let us go down and confuse their language so they will not understand each other.' So the LORD scattered them from there over all the earth, and they stopped building the city. That is why it was called Babel – because there the LORD confused the language of the whole world. From there the LORD scattered them over the face of the whole earth (Genesis 11:1–9).

On the face of it, this story does seem to imply that human cultural and linguistic diversity was not part of the divine intention for humanity, and that it only came about as a result of divine judgement upon an enterprise that was designed primarily for the sake of status and prestige. If this is the case then we may assume that diversity, and the pluralist outlook that seeks to accommodate it, are not things that would meet with God's approval.

But before we come to that conclusion, we should remember that the divine mandate given to humanity was to 'fill the earth and subdue it'. This scattering is fairly evident in the 'Table of Nations' in Genesis 10. One inevitable outcome of such a process would be the emergence of distinct and diverse cultures and languages, which are in fact referred to several times in that chapter, that is, before the story of Babel (Genesis 10:4, 20, 31).

In the Babel story, the problem is not only that the enterprise was founded and focused on human reputation. The plan was that they would 'not be scattered over the face of the whole earth', that is, in direct contravention of the original divine intention. Ironically, the outcome of the multiplication of languages was exactly the sort of scattering that the protagonists had tried to prevent. The contrast with a later biblical story involving another tower is instructive. Jacob's so-called 'ladder' at Bethel (Genesis 28:10–18) was probably the staircase of a Babylonian ziggurat, a stepped pyramid (which is also what is in mind with regard to Babel's 'tower') at the top of which the gods were assumed to dwell. And God's promise to Jacob at Bethel was that his innumerable descendants would 'spread out to the west and to the east, to the north and to the south' (Genesis 28:14), in marked contrast to the intention of the engineers of Babel.

Human migration seems to be a biblical and historical norm. Israel was encouraged to recognize, through confessions like 'My father was a wandering Aramean' (Deuteronomy 26:5), not only its own experiences of wandering in the desert of Sinai, but also its earlier roots in the nomadism of the patriarchs. Awareness of other such migrations is echoed in the historical parentheses of Deuteronomy 2:10–12, 20–23 and in prophetic utterances such as Amos 9:7. Even the nationalistic 'blood and land' theology of Acts 17:26 does not preclude the interpretation that, if God decides where each nation should live, he is also more than able to decide when they should move. Salman Rushdie suggests that:

To explain why we become attached to our birthplaces we pretend that we are trees and speak of roots. Look under your feet. You will not find gnarled growths spouting through the soles. Roots, I sometimes think, are a conservative myth designed to keep us in our places.[8]

God's intervention at Babel served not only to 'help' humanity in fulfilling its original mandate to scatter and diversify, but also served a preventative role, hindering human hubris and status seeking, in effect protecting us from ourselves. The story of Babel is best seen not only as an expression of God's judgement, but of his mercy. Cultural diversification may therefore be a sign of God's judgement upon universalizing, homogenizing forces. It is a sign of his mercy and grace that these do not prevail, and that he will act to uphold his original creation intention of diversity and variation.

Pentecost is often interpreted as an undoing of the judgement of Babel. The important thing to note is that God did not restore a single human language. Instead, those present heard the wonders of God being declared *in their own languages*. Perhaps Pentecost itself was another judgement on homogenizing tendencies. For at that time people had to travel to Jerusalem from across the known world (from Persia to Libya, Arabia to Rome [Acts 2:9–11]) in order to worship God in a single place, and were only able to communicate through the common trade language of Greek (or,

> **The single language was the curse – the multiplicity of languages is the blessing.**
>
> *Fearghas MacFhionnlaigh*[9]

---

[8] Salman Rushdie, *Shame* (New York: Vintage, 1984), p. 91.

[9] Fearghas MacFhionnlaigh, 'Creative Tensions', *Scottish Bulletin of Evangelical Theology* 14/1 (Spring 1996), p. 39.

if they were lucky, in the local dialect of Aramaic). Their experience at Pentecost was the polar opposite of the expected norm.

Dewi Hughes has noted that 'empire building always involves a drive towards linguistic and cultural uniformity'.[10] In his classic book *1984* George Orwell explored the totalitarian drive towards such uniformity:

> The purpose of Newspeak was not only to provide a medium of expression for the world-view and mental habits proper to the devotees of Ingsoc, but to make all other modes of thought impossible. It was intended that when Newspeak had been adopted once and for all and Oldspeak forgotten, a heretical thought – that is, a thought diverging from the principles of Ingsoc – should literally be unthinkable, at least so far as thought is dependent upon words. Its vocabulary was so constructed as to give exact and very subtle expression to every meaning that a party member could properly wish to express, while excluding all other meanings ... To give a single example. The word *free* still existed in Newspeak, but it could only be used in statements such as 'this dog is free from lice' and 'this field is free from weeds'. It could not be used in its old sense of 'politically free' or 'intellectually free', since political and intellectual freedom no longer existed even as concepts, and were therefore of necessity nameless.[11]

And so while specific human cultures may be a complex mixture of good and bad, cultural diversity in itself is something to be prized, cherished and enhanced. While it is

---

[10] Dewi Hughes, *'Castrating Culture: A Christian Perspective on Ethnic Identity from the Margins* (Carlisle: Paternoster Press, 2001), p. 68.

[11] George Orwell, *1984* (Harmondsworth: Penguin, 1967), pp. 241–2.

dangerous to think of globalization and postmodernity as 'the work of God in history', they are trends to be welcomed, in so far as they are reflections of the diversity that God intends for humanity. The Scottish Gaelic poet Fearghas MacFhionnlaigh would agree:

> The single language of Babel is refracted into the many. Why? To deliver us from the tyranny of pagan thought-control which a monopolistic world language threatens. To deliver us from the silence which totalitarianism always seeks to impose on the populace in its grip. God leads the jailbreak. For freedom Christ has set us free, free to seek God while he may be found and where he may be found (though he is not far from any of us). And each language is a searchlight with which to seek him. A fissure, a hole punched in the wall of silence.[12]

More than a mosaic

There has been an increasing interest in contextualization in recent years in the global missionary movement, although perhaps more in academic missiological circles than by the average missionary him- or herself. Cultural anthropology now features in missionary training curricula and missionaries are encouraged to be aware of their own cultural conditioning as they work among people of very different cultures. In such thinking, cultures are often viewed as autonomous wholes, each forming a single piece in a global mosaic of peoples and cultures. Beliefs, values and behaviours are perceived to cohere in an integrated fashion, and to make sense.

This approach is inevitable for a number of reasons. First, most of us think that we are more consistent than we really are, especially when our experience of life is generally

[12] MacFhionnlaigh, 'Creative Tensions', p. 45.

secure and meaningful, and our actions and beliefs seem to make sense. Robert Schreiter points out that those who have lived fairly contented lives and who have not ventured out much beyond the confines of their culture are rarely drawn to ask fundamental questions about the assumptions upon which their lives, expectations and experiences are based.[13] Secondly, such models have dominated anthropological thinking since its inception in the nineteenth century and have been reinforced by the need to find situations of manageable size for study purposes (so that small, discrete, coherent and relatively isolated social and cultural groups have been favoured by such studies).

The problem is that, apart from a relatively small number of tribes located in the Amazon rainforest and the backwaters of the larger islands of the Pacific Ocean, such as Papua New Guinea, such groups are really rather thin on the ground. Human history has generally been much more about interaction, mingling, adaptation and resistance between different villages, towns, tribes, regions, kingdoms, nations and empires. This has gone on since well before the time of Christ, when ancient metropolises like Alexandria in Egypt were a melting pot for ideas, where, for example, early Buddhist thought influenced the development of Greek philosophy. Beliefs and practices that a group believes to be theirs by long tradition often turn out to be of relatively recent adoption. In 1970 the Nyole people of eastern Uganda referred to their practice of growing cotton as a traditional way of subsistence, whereas it was in fact introduced by the British early in the twentieth century.[14] And, as we have seen, because of globalization this kind of intercultural exchange and flow is accelerating rapidly, both with

---

[13] Robert J. Schreiter, *The New Catholicity: Theology between the Global and the Local* (Maryknoll, New York: Orbis, 1997), p. 48.

[14] Finnström, 'Postcoloniality and the Postcolony'.

increased physical migration and through the stream of symbols, images and text we receive via the media. In such a context, the number of people who live the kind of bounded, secure lives referred to above is reducing, and most, if not all of us, are now forced to acknowledge the existence of radically different beliefs and lifestyles from our own.

The winners and losers experience this assault on integrated culture differently, and yet they are also affected similarly by it. For the world's poor and its migrant populations, life has long offered little or no coherent security. Even those for whom globalization is a positive thing (for example, the consumers of Europe and North America) also experience major challenges to their comfortable insularity through the presence of large immigrant communities, often from former colonies, in their countries. Fear of crime, of employment insecurity, and of the 'other', characterize large segments of public opinion in many European countries. The disappearance of any common ground in society leads either to fragmentation or to the production of a multiculturalism that tries to make sense of the visible and rapid differentiation of society. This really is a situation where 'the empire strikes back', as the former colonizers experience some of the insecurity and disruption that they imposed on those they colonized in a previous era.

A good example of the variety of cultural flows that can impact even a relatively remote location is the island of Misima, which is located off the eastern end of Papua New Guinea.[15] The flow of past and present cultural influences upon the island is astounding. Misimans are involved in regional trade with its neighbouring islands of Calvados, Sudest and Rossel, as well as with the nearby Kula islands and with trading systems on the main island of Papua New

---

[15] Michael A. Rynkiewich, 'The World in my Parish: Rethinking the Standard Missiological Model', *Missiology: An International Review* 30/3 (July 2002), pp. 301–21.

Guinea. More recent trading influences include South Pacific Beer, Korean-run stores and an Australian–Canadian gold mine. Early missionary work was done by the Methodists, followed since the Second World War by the Sacred Heart Mission, Seventh-Day Adventists, Jehovah's Witnesses, Wycliffe Bible Translators, Operation Mobilisation, Kenneth Hagin, Morris Cerullo, Benny Hinn and many, many others. By observing the way that islanders adopt, adapt and interact with these many and varied inputs, Michael Rynkiewich states that 'in reality, the current missionary situation far more resembles the floor of the New York Stock Exchange five minutes before closing time than a quiet table for two at the secluded café down the street'.[16] Each culture is a complex mosaic in itself, with new pieces continually being added, old pieces being lost, and an often-unseemly squabble going on about who gets to decide which pieces get to stay and where, and which have to go. In Misima as much as in Tunisia, each culture is in itself an ever-recreating mosaic.

> **Culture is produced through history and the processes of syncretism and hybridization it spawns ...**
>
> *Aletta Biersack*[17]

This process of culture creating is not simply a contemporary phenomenon. Some of the larger tribal groups in Africa have come about through homogenizing processes instituted by colonial administrations. This reality contradicts the 'essentializing' assumptions of some models of culture and ethnicity, wherein culture is seen as a primordial given, a

16 Ibid., p. 304.
17 Quoted in ibid., p. 306.

fixed and immutable reality. The cultural identities are often no less real and heartfelt for being so created, but we should not make the mistake of assuming that culture and identity is fixed, as some missionary strategists have done. Those concerned with identifying and targeting the remaining 'unreached people groups' of the world may find themselves frustrated as cultural identities shift, merge and emerge anew. The targets just won't stay still.

Examples of the creation of tribal identities include the Yoruba of Nigeria, the Sukuma of Tanzania and (perhaps the bitterest irony) the Hutu and Tutsi of Rwanda/Burundi. The Sukuma of Tanzania were first categorized as a single tribe by the colonial authorities in East Africa. 'Rather fluid social entities were given a more defined identity under the label of tribe'[18] in colonial documents, and a variety of Sukuma dialects were standardized through the translation of the Bible and through language teaching in missionary schools. The long-term outcome of such processes is a homogenization of previously existing diversity.

In Rwanda and Burundi, agricultural and pastoral peoples shared the same land, the same language, and to a large extent the same social world, although there were strong, caste-like distinctions, with the pastoralist Tutsis being seen as superior to the farming Hutus. The Belgian colonial authorities solidified these distinctions by simplistically defining those who owned more than ten cattle as Tutsi, and the rest as Hutu.

Such categorizations were not always the result of colonial interference. While the Yoruba are now rightly understood as one of the major ethnic groups of modern Nigeria, occupying much of the south-western portion of

---

[18] Per Brandström, 'Who is a Sukuma and Who is a Nyamwezi? Ethnic Identity in West-Central Tanzania', Working Papers in African Studies #27, Department of Cultural Anthropology, University of Uppsala (1986), p. 4.

the country, the term was originally used by others to describe a number of semi-independent peoples loosely linked by language, geography, history and culture, who spent as much time fighting with each other as with their neighbours:

> Until relatively recent times the Yoruba did not consider them-selves a single people, but rather as citizens of Oyo, Benin, Yagba and other cities, regions or kingdoms. These cities regarded Lagos and Owo, for example, as foreign neighbours, and the Yoruba kingdoms warred not only against the Dahomeans but also against each other. The name Yoruba was applied to all these linguistically and culturally related peoples by their northern neighbours, the Hausas.[19]

Mixing it up

Cultural purity was probably always a myth, but it is now less tenable than ever. The global spread of sounds and images through radio, TV, cinema, VCR, DVD and the Internet provides new cultural resources to previously bounded cultures. Combined with the huge global migra-tions of people that have and are taking place, cultures are now more accurately described as deterritorialized, hyper-differentiated and hybridized.[20] Cultures are deterritorial-ized to the extent that they can no longer be exclusively assigned to certain places or regions. In many of the world's major cities different cultures co-exist and jostle for space. Hyperdifferentiation signifies the different worlds that a single person inhabits at the same time, simultaneously belonging to different 'realities'. So my Pakistani neighbour who works as an accountant for a satellite TV company

---

[19] See < www.cultural-expressions.com/ifa/ifahistory.htm >.
[20] Schreiter, *The New Catholicity*, pp. 26–7.

occupies one cultural world (characterized by Western dress, values and priorities) during his working life, and another in his home, where Urdu, the shalwar kameez and Punjabi food are the norm. And he was born in England. Finally, cultures are increasingly hybridized, mixing and creating new cultural forms as they go along. Just as rock 'n' roll can be characterized as 'black music played by white people' and mambo as coming from a fusion of black and Latin styles, so Bhangra rap provides evidence of black-Asian cultural cross-fertilization. The crossover successes of singers and musicians like Ricky Martin, Jennifer Lopez and Carlos Santana show that there is a strong Latin impact on Anglo musical culture and tastes. Colombian singer Shakira even manages to provide an Afro-punk version of one of her hits.

Hybridity as a term has had a bad press because of its use in nineteenth-century scientific-racist discussions. At that time it was seen as a bad thing, to be avoided if possible, since mixed-race births were held to 'dilute' racial purity. Homi Bhabha has sought to rehabilitate the term, writing about an 'empowering hybridity' that exists in those intercultural encounters where cultural differences are allowed to co-exist. Other terms that have been used to describe cultural intermingling are creolization and mestizo. Creolization is a process, not an outcome, and often results in unconscious forms of hybridity. It is usually applied to Caribbean societies, or more loosely to other ethnically or racially mixed populations that are a product of European colonization. And in no way is the cultural traffic all one-way:

> This imitation [of the master] went on, naturally, most easily among those in closest and most intimate contact with Europeans, among that is, domestic slaves, female slaves with white lovers, slaves in contact with missionaries or traders or

sailors, skilled slaves anxious to deploy their skills, and above all, among urban slaves in contact with the 'wider' life ... But it was a two-way process, and it worked both ways. In white households the Negro influence was pervasive, especially in the country areas. To preserve the pure dialect of the tribe (at least of the females) planters had to send to England for governesses and practically locked their daughters away from Negro influence. But it was in the intimate area of sexual relationships that the greatest damage was done to white creole apartheid policy and where the most significant – and lasting – intercultural creolization took place.[21]

The term mestizo has its origins in the older large-scale Spanish and Portuguese settlement of Meso- and South America. This was characterized by intensive cultural and racial interchange between settlers and native peoples (often before the advent and influence of black slaves into the cultural mix) and can be seen as a positive national sign of shared indigeneity, since such mixing and independence often both occurred relatively early. The mestizo identity has moved away from pejorative associations towards more positive ones since the recognition that such interchange has produced new and powerful synergistic cultural forms and that the most energetic aspects of the new cultures reside at the boundaries of ethnic, racial and cultural exchange. This is the case for much popular music and also for literature. Writers such as V.S. Naipaul, Salman Rushdie and Chinua Achebe are widely respected, and part of their talent resides in their distinctive perspective from within cultures that have experienced colonization:

---

[21] Edward Kamau Brathwaite, 'Creolization in Jamaica' in B. Ashcroft, Gareth Griffiths and Helen Tiffin, *The Postcolonial Studies Reader* (London: Routledge, 1995), p. 203.

We lived at the crossroads of cultures. We still do today; but when I was a boy one could see and sense the peculiar quality and atmosphere of it more clearly. I am not talking about all that rubbish we hear, of the spiritual void and mental stresses that Africans are supposed to have, or the evil forces and irrational passions prowling through Africa's heart of darkness. We know the racist mystique behind a lot of that stuff and should merely point out that those who prefer to see Africa in those lurid terms have not themselves demonstrated any clear superiority in sanity or competence in coping with life. But still the crossroads does have a certain dangerous potency; dangerous because a man might perish there wrestling with multiple-headed spirits, but he also might be lucky and return to his people with the boon of prophetic vision.[22]

Concluding thoughts

So far we have seen how cultural diversification is a present reality, and it is, I would suggest, part of the divine intention for humanity. Business is brisk on the cultural trading floor, and in so far as it leads to creativity and new cultural forms this is something to be welcomed. Of course, not all cultural interchanges can be characterized as good-natured sharing. Culture can also be used to resist domination or intrusion, as we saw earlier in the McWorld/Jihad formulation.

These considerations have serious implications for the missionary practice of contextualization. Culture is increasingly becoming a political issue, especially in places that are located on the boundaries of two or more cultures (in other words, most places). To contextualize the gospel into a particular cultural form is to make a statement about that

---

[22] Chinua Achebe, 'Named for Victoria, Queen of England' in Ashcroft ey al., *The Postcolonial Studies Reader*, p. 190 ff.

culture and about those other cultures that are resisting or interacting with it. To pretend that you can avoid this dilemma by ignoring it is to make a decision none the less. As Jonathan Ingleby points out, 'accepting the cultural status quo usually means siding with the dominant culture'.[23] In fact, there is a strong case to be made that part of the missionary role is to 'preserve' or possibly to 'prefer' certain cultures. Note again what Ingleby says: 'Contexts are not uniform. The gospel is not neutral. It tilts mission towards the poor.'[24] This is as true for those who are considered culturally marginalized as for those who are economically marginalized. A strong commitment to cultural diversity must allow room for the margins to prosper and for new cultural forms to emerge, for this is, as we have seen, part of the divine intention for humanity.

---

[23] Jonathan Ingleby, 'Trickling Down or Shaking the Foundations: Is Contextualization Neutral?', *Missiology* 25/2 (April 1997), p. 185.

[24] Ibid.

Intermezzo

This point marks something of a break within the book. Until now we have been considering global trends of diversification and a Christian response to them. We now turn to the subject of the mission agency, which has been so significant an actor in the 200-year life of the modern Protestant missionary movement to date. How can mission agencies be helped to thrive at the global pick 'n' mix counter?

Chapter 4

Creaking at the Seams

Where did it all go wrong for mission agencies?

You don't have to read far in some contemporary writing about world mission before you encounter a sense of pessimism. Granted, missionary magazines and journals produced for consumption by supporters tend to report on the positive outcomes of an organization's activities, so as to solicit continued giving to an organization's work. But once you scratch beneath the surface one finds that many mission agencies are finding life increasingly difficult. No word is too strong, it seems, to describe the difficulties faced by mission agencies:

> More than ever before in its history, the Christian mission is in the firing line today.[1]

> The crisis of identity that many long-established Western missionary societies are facing today …[2]

> A missions agency mired in an effectiveness crisis …[3]

---

[1] Bosch, *Transforming Mission*, p. 2. The subtitle given to the section from which this quotation is taken is 'Mission: The Contemporary Crisis'.

[2] Wilbert Shenk, *Changing Frontiers of Mission* (Maryknoll, New York: Orbis, 1999), p. 177.

[3] James F. Engel and William A. Dyrness, *Changing the Mind of Missions: Where have we Gone Wrong?* (Downers Grove, Illinois: InterVarsity Press, 2000), p. 17.

My experience of the UK evangelical world mission scene over the past ten years, six of which were spent working as a director of Global Connections, the network/umbrella/'trade association' for the sector, certainly confirms that the modern Western missionary movement is facing a series of challenges and tensions. There is a widespread sense that the old ways of doing things, and the structures that served them, no longer fit the new realities of the twenty-first century.

So, apart from the issues of globalization and post-modernity, what other 'new realities' are leading to this sense of crisis?

Jeux sans frontieres?

One of the other important changes affecting the Western missionary movement is the growth of the church around the world in the last fifty years and the decline in church attendance in the West during the same period. Wilbert Shenk has suggested that mission should be understood as action at the 'frontier' between faith and unfaith.[4] When Europe and its various colonial offshoots (now known collectively as 'the West') still largely viewed themselves as 'Christian' it was relatively easily to decide where these frontiers were. All you had to do was look at a map – if it wasn't in the West, then it was a place where 'mission' happened. The various versions of the mission agency that have emerged over the past 200 years have largely been based on this assumption. But with the church now being a global phenomenon, growing rapidly in many places (but most definitely not in the West), drawing the frontier is no longer an easy task.

Global migration and a fluid and changing religious map now mean that most places can be considered as 'frontiers'. There are no real centres or Christian 'heartlands'. Shenk's

---

[4] Shenk, *Changing Frontiers of Mission*, p. 183.

concept of 'changing frontiers' has shaped a discussion about where the new frontiers of mission might be, in order to help mission agencies to reorient themselves. After all, if the frontiers have changed, then organizations formed to face one particular set of frontiers might end up facing the wrong way!

In *Mission after Christendom*[5] David Smith suggests that the three most challenging frontiers for mission are the frontiers of secularization, pluralization and globalization. Shenk provides his own detailed shopping list, including materialism, hedonism, nationalism, racism, sexism, new religions, environmental degradation and more.[6] No one can deny the need for a sustained and creative missionary strategy to engage the post-Christian West. But I question whether many mission agencies will be able to reorient themselves to face these new frontiers, even if they wanted to. The specific cultural expertise of their personnel, as well as their funding patterns and expectations, makes the likely success of such a manoeuvre improbable. There are not many Lesslie Newbigins in this world; that is, those that are able to take the cross-cultural expertise they have acquired in one context and apply it to another. Some will be able to make the transition, but most, I suggest, will not.

Nor can it be reasonably argued that the growth of the church worldwide invalidates the need for further continued input by Western churches and mission agencies into traditional 'fields' of work, nor for numerous new missionary initiatives in regions dominated by Islam, Hinduism and Buddhism. While the days of Western dominance in global mission are surely now behind us, and their work is done alongside those from other parts of the world, there is still a significant role for Western churches and mission agencies to play in Christian mission outside the West:

[5] David Smith, *Mission after Christendom* (London: Darton, Longman & Todd, 2003).

[6] Shenk, *Changing Frontiers of Mission*, p. 184.

The reality is that the heritage, the resources, the people, the training institutions, and the money, are still strongly Western. How can Western mission agencies respond in tandem with what God is doing in bringing the church, and the centre of Christianity, to Africa, Latin America and Asia?[7]

If the Western church really ceases to dominate global Christianity, does this mean that its missionary responsibility disappears? Mission should be understood as a mark of the church, not simply as the foreign policy of a vibrant Christendom. If we truly believe that mission should be done in weakness, then a weakened Western church would in fact be better fitted for missionary involvement than hitherto.

We must, however, acknowledge that the mission agency is ceasing to be the only or even the 'normal' means by which individuals become involved in cross-cultural mission. Many other forms of involvement now offer themselves:

Real international missionary growth is in majority-world churches, short-term missions, tentmaking, bivocational and non-residential missions. We must begin to teach about, and give access to new models of mission. In this area, we need to foster multiple visions of the future and allow for creativity. We should explore other models of mission – intentionally calling individuals to work with multi-national corporations, to tentmaking organizations founded by missionary believers, to NGOs, the PeaceCorp, relief and development models, ethnic minority models, study abroad as mission work, even tourism and micromission.[8]

---

[7] Kang San Tan (OMF Malaysia), 'Interview', *Global Connections Newsletter* (September 2002), p. 3.

[8] Paula Harris, 'Renewing Urbana', unpublished internal paper (March 2003), p. 3.

Personally, I think that talk of a 'crisis in Christian mission' is excessive. To use that language may be to confuse the challenges faced by some Western mission agencies with the future of the Western (and even global) missionary movement as a whole. Some mission agencies certainly face severe challenges to organizational effectiveness, and even to survival. A number of organizations are facing these challenges with a spirit of creativity and innovation, whereas others are still trying to work out what changes to make. Some might not even be aware of the need to change, and would resist it if they knew.

The future of the mission agency

I do not think that Western mission agencies should be written off as an anachronism. The knowledge, expertise and organizational learning bound up in those organizations will remain a vital asset to be drawn on by Western local churches, if the cross-cultural mission involvement of the latter is not to result simply in a series of square, rectangular and hexagonal wheels.[9] And, if I am right in my analysis of the implications of globalization and postmodernity, that is, that options and variety will increase rather than decrease, then in no way will world mission become the sole or even primary prerogative of the local church, or of any single other way of doing mission. Individuals will still join mission agencies, new organizations will continue to be formed and entirely new ways of doing mission will also develop.

But we have already noted that mission agencies are facing a number of other changes apart from the rising prominence of the local church. Many of these are not

---

[9] It is, after all, hard to improve on the original design.

unique to mission agencies. All organizations are products of their time, and for mission agencies this includes not only the 'frontiers' toward which they are directed, but also their organizational cultures and ways of working, since 'mission structures necessarily entail the application of human institutional forms. Structures devised for mission will thus always be susceptible to the same faults and distortions that beset their secular counterparts.'[10]

To understand this more clearly, we will look at the origins of the modern mission agency, the organizational assumptions and models upon which it is based, and the social and cultural changes that are affecting the viability of these models for the future. This will provide us with ideas and a road map for helping mission agencies to change and thrive in the twenty-first century.

Where did mission agencies come from?

When the founders of the Baptist Missionary Society, the London Missionary Society and the Church Missionary Society were making their initial plans in the late eighteenth century, they were not working in a vacuum. William Carey's famous tract gave away its intention by its title – 'An Enquiry into the Obligation of Christians to Use Means for the Conversion of the Heathens'. Those 'means' already existed in the wider society of the time, in the form of the voluntary association or society.

The voluntary society

The voluntary society began as a peculiarly Protestant form of social organization. The spirit of enterprise and initiative

[10] Stanley H. Skreslet, 'Impending Transformation: Mission Structures for a New Century', *International Bulletin of Missionary Research* 23/1 (January 1999), p. 2.

fostered by the Enlightenment, combined with the Reformation principle of the right to private interpretation of the Bible, led to the idea that individuals could also band together in common cause and interest. Many of the earliest voluntary associations remained part of the Church of England and had close links to the existing ecclesiastical structures (The Society for the Propagation of the Gospel and Society for Promoting Christian Knowledge are two such examples). John Wesley had made use of these concepts in the development of the movement (also initially within the Church of England) that became known as Methodism.

By the early nineteenth century the idea had expanded beyond these limits and was put to wider use. Voluntary associations were established for the purposes of missionary enterprise, Bible production and distribution, banning slavery, prison reform, temperance and myriad other purposes. In 1830 French aristocrat Alexis de Tocqueville visited America and was deeply impressed by the American propensity for voluntary associations:

> Americans of all ages, all stations in life, and all types of disposition, are forever forming associations. There are not only commercial and industrial associations in which all take part, but others of a thousand different types – religious, moral, serious, futile, very general and very limited, immensely large and very minute. Nothing, in my view, deserves more attention than the intellectual and moral associations of America.[11]

The relative social and political egalitarianism of the emerging democracies of Europe and North America allowed

---

[11] Quoted by Robert Putnam, 'Bowling Alone: America's Declining Social Capital', *Journal of Democracy* 6/1 (January 1995), pp. 65–6. Available at < muse.jhu.edu/demo/journal_of_democracy/v006/putnam.html >.

for wide ownership of and commitment to such societies.[12] Networks of auxiliary associations raised funds and sent them to a central office, receiving back information for prayer and action. Involvement was open to all social classes:

> What we see in Missionary, Bible, Tract and other kindred societies, not restricted to ecclesiastics, nor to any one profession, but combining all classes, embracing the masses of the people; and all free, open, and responsible ... It is the contributors of the funds who are the real association, the individuals, churches, congregations, who freely act together through such agencies for an object of common interest.[13]

The use of the principle of voluntary association by many missionary societies is well recognized.[14] It provided a model upon which to structure their work and has proved to be remarkably effective and flexible over 200 years of mission history. Evangelicalism, with its individualistic spirituality, its distrust of official church structures and its methods of group discipleship, has found it easy to use such structures and systems. As the first missionary societies were absorbed into their denominations of origin by the middle of the nineteenth century, a new generation of mission agencies based on the voluntary principle came into

---

[12] As well as the eighteenth-century British examples mentioned above, some other early missionary societies included the American Board of Commissioners for Foreign Missions (1810), the Basle Mission (1815) and the Berlin Society (1824).

[13] Rufus Anderson, *The Time for the World's Conversion Come* (1837) quoted in Andrew Walls, *The Missionary Movement in Christian History* (Edinburgh: T. & T. Clark, 1996), p. 242.

[14] See, for example, Bosch, *Transforming Mission*, pp. 327–34; Stephen Neill, *A History of Christian Missions* (London: Penguin, 1986²), p. 214; Shenk, *Changing Frontiers of Mission*, pp. 178–9; Walls, *The Missionary Movement in Christian History*, pp. 241–54.

being to work in the 'inland' areas hitherto neglected by the older societies. The principle was invoked again in the formation of a new wave of evangelical mission agencies in the decades after the Second World War.

But perhaps what is less well acknowledged is that patterns of social affiliation are changing at this point in time, with significant implications for Christian mission agencies.

Bowling alone

In 1995 an article entitled 'Bowling Alone: America's Declining Social Capital', by Harvard professor Robert Putnam, was published in the *Journal of Democracy*.[15] The article aroused so much interest that a book later followed.[16] Putnam's thesis was that the networks of social and civic engagement (or 'voluntary societies') described by Tocqueville were in decline. He quotes a staggering array of statistics showing that across all types of social association, such as religious affiliation (church attendance), union membership, participation in parent-teacher associations and the number of volunteers for civic organizations such as the Boys Scouts and the Red Cross, involvement has declined in the last fifty years. The title of his article came from his discovery that, while more Americans go tenpin bowling than ever, participation in organized bowling leagues fell 40 per cent between 1980 and 1993.

Putnam mentions Tocqueville's observations about the American propensity to associate and notes that social networks and civic engagement of the kind he describes have been shown to have a powerful influence on economic

---

[15] For publication details, see footnote 10.
[16] Putnam, *Bowling Alone*.

attainment, poverty, unemployment, the control of crime and drug abuse, education and even health. This, he argues, shows the importance of high levels of social capital, a term which refers to 'features of social organization such as networks, norms, and social trust that facilitate coordination and cooperation for mutual benefit'.[17]

This is not a trend that affects America alone. A decline in the level of social engagement in Europe is also evident, argues Putnam, even if it is not as clear and unambiguous as in the USA,[18] and levels of social capital are far lower in Britain than in most of the rest of Europe.[19]

Before we decry the rampant individualism and the breakdown of society reflected in these figures, we should note that other forms of civic and social association have emerged to replace these older structures. Mass-membership organizations such as the National Trust, Greenpeace and the giant American Association of Retired Persons (AARP)[20] have grown rapidly since the 1970s. Similarly, gym membership is now one of the most common forms of social affiliation for younger generations, and we should note the importance assigned to small groups and networks of friends and associates made through work.

But we can also note that these newer forms of social affiliation are different from the earlier voluntary societies.

Robert Wuthnow notes that 40 per cent of all Americans claim to be 'currently involved in a small group that meets regularly and provides support or caring for those who

---

[17] Robert D Putnam, 'Bowling Alone', p. 67.

[18] Robert D. Putnam, 'Let's Play Together', *The Observer*, 25 March 2001. Available from < http://www.observer.co.uk/comment/story/0,6903,462665,00.html >.

[19] Polly Toynbee, 'A Whole Nation of Meldrews: I Just Can't Believe It', *The Guardian*, 28 August 2002. Available from < www.guardian.co.uk/comment/story/0,3604,781684,00.html >.

[20] Membership of 35 million in 1996.

participate in it'.[21] This includes Bible study groups and prayer fellowships, Alcoholics Anonymous meetings, book discussion groups and hobby clubs. These small groups often move beyond their initial purpose into wider community involvement, as well as acting as a substitute for other relationship ties that have been weakened in a fragmented society (divorced and single people are two to four times more likely to be involved in small groups). However, such groups can often be fluid in membership, and the networking propensities of younger generations rarely, if ever, cut across social boundaries.

Mass-membership organizations are based on commitment to a common symbol or ideal, or to common benefits, and not generally on commitment to work with other people. Little in the way of action is expected by such an organization's members, except perhaps the payment of annual dues and the receipt of a newsletter:

> Only 5 to 10 percent of AARP members participate in local affiliates, and new members join after getting a letter in the mail, not an invitation to a local club meeting. The AARP is not like the locally rooted federations that once dominated the ranks of nationwide US voluntary associations.[22]

This does not mean that such organizations are unable to have an impact. But they are often seen as acting 'on behalf of' their members, rather than being a conduit through which their members' concerns can be channelled. Such 'members' might be better understood as 'consumers' of a cause, and are best likened to fans rather than players. Symbolic affiliation of this nature translates into low levels of loyalty, which is inevitable when individual participation is reduced to the level of simply writing an occasional cheque. Direct mail becomes a key method of membership and income growth for such organizations and dropout

rates after the first year average around 30 per cent. Involvement levels are volatile and unpredictable. For example,
Greenpeace grew in membership from 800,000 to 2.35
million between 1985–1990 and then fell by 85 per cent to
around 350,000 by 1998.[23]

Voluntary associations began their existence as a way
that individuals and groups committed to a common cause
could act together and have ended up as organizations that
do so on behalf of them.

What are the causes of these changes in voluntary association and of declining levels of social capital? Putnam
explores a number of alternatives, including the movement
of women into the labour force and increased social and
physical mobility, and concludes that these are not likely to
be major contributory factors. More significant, he believes,
are demographic transformations in the family and also
the change of scale in the urban environment, such as the
replacement of local community-based firms with retail out-
lets that are outposts of distant multinational corporations.
Most significant of all, he suggests, is what he calls the
'technological transformation of leisure', by which he means
the TV, the VCR and the video game, all of which have
individualized us and reduced our integration within our
communities. All of these have the biggest impact on
younger generations, since 'epochal watersheds have their
biggest influence on the outlooks of young adults'.[24]

Ultimately, the causes of the changes tracked by Putnam
are less relevant than the question of whether we can do

---

[21]   Putnam, *Bowling Alone*, p. 148 ff.

[22]   Theda Skocpol, 'Unravelling from Above', *The American
    Prospect* 7/25 (March 1996), pp. 20–25. Available at < www.
    prospect.org/print/V7/25/25-cnt2.html >.

[23]   Putnam, *Bowling Alone*, pp. 155, 158.

[24]   Skocpol, 'Unravelling from Above', quoting social scientist
    Karl Mannheim.

anything about them: is the voluntary association doomed to wither and die? There are some signs of hope, suggesting that this is an issue of change rather than of extinction. For example, Putnam sees networks as the most productive forms of social capital (rather than, for example, more formal associations). Loosely based structures are more efficient than those that are closely knit organizations with high membership boundaries (which Putnam suggests are prone to 'inefficient cartelization and rent-seeking, or what ordinary men and women call corruption').[25] We will look at networks in more detail later in this book.

What are the implications of these trends for mission agencies? If we accept that the mission agency owes something of its origin to the emergence of the 'voluntary society' then it is inevitable that changes in the nature of social affiliation will have an impact upon any organization based on such models. Because the voluntary society had a vital feature: 'it depended on its very existence on regular participation; it developed means of gaining that participation at local level ... a network of locally organised auxiliary associations.'[26]

The wide sense of ownership and involvement inculcated by the successful voluntary society is being replaced on the one hand by a much looser sense of affiliation to and ownership of large causes and on the other hand by closer relationships and loyalties to one's immediate group of friends and contacts. The network is replacing the membership organization as the voluntary society of the twenty-first century. Perhaps the much-lamented 'loss of commitment' to mission agencies by younger generations is more of a social issue than a theological one. And perhaps the problem is not so

---

[25] Putnam, 'Bowling Alone', p. 75.
[26] Walls, *The Missionary Movement in Christian History*, pp. 250–1.

much with the 'younger generation'; instead it is located in the desire of some organizations to continue to work with outdated structures that are being undermined by wider social trends.

The tendency of voluntary organizations to 'professionalize' and act 'on behalf of' their members, rather than through them, becomes even more evident when we look at the specific type of voluntary society that was consciously adopted by the early mission agencies: that is, the joint-stock trading company.

The joint-stock trading company

When a trading company has obtained its charter, they usually go to its utmost limits; and their stocks, their ships, their officers and men are so chosen and regulated as to be likely to answer their purpose; but they do not stop there, for encouraged by the prospect of success they use every effort, cast their bread upon the waters, cultivate friendship with everyone from whose information they expect the least advantage.

Suppose a company of serious Christians, ministers and private persons, were to form themselves into a society, and make a number of rules respecting the regulation of the plan, and the persons who are to be employed as missionaries, the means of defraying the expenses, etc, etc.

From such a society a committee might be appointed, whose business it should be to procure all the information they could upon the subject, to receive contributions, to enquire into the characters, tempers, abilities and religious views of the missionaries, and also to provide them with necessaries for their undertakings.[27]

---

[27] William Carey, 'An Enquiry into the Obligation of Christians to Use Means for the Conversion of the Heathens' (1792) in

The voluntary society may have become common by the 1830s, but as little as forty years earlier, when William Carey wrote the above words, it was still very much in its infancy. Such associations could in fact be viewed with extreme suspicion given the nature of the times. English Dissenters like Carey were sometimes thought to have revolutionary aims hidden under the cloak of 'religious and civil liberty', and foreign missions were opposed in some quarters, such as in the General Assembly of the Church of Scotland, because of such associations. And so Carey took his specific analogy from the world of business – organizing a missionary society is something like floating a company – thus providing a safer model that would be acceptable to a wider body of opinion.

It is doubtful that Carey intended the metaphor of the joint-stock company to be taken literally or pressed to the full extent of its meaning. He intended that his work should be led and managed from India. But the later move of the Baptist Missionary Society from Kettering to London and the emergence of new leadership that wanted to institute full business procedures and full control of field operations sowed the seeds of the ultimate split between Carey and the organization that he was instrumental in founding.

And the business analogy, while fortuitous, also had an unforeseen formative role in shaping the organizational future of the mission agency.[28] It was largely positive, taking advantage of powerful social currents flowing at the time. The Industrial Revolution in Britain provided for increased

---

[27] (*continued*) Ralph D. Winter and Stephen C. Hawthorne (eds), *Perspectives on the World Christian Movement* (Carlisle: Paternoster Press, 1992²), B–101–2.

[28] For a fuller treatment of this theme, see Dwight P. Baker, 'William Carey and the Business Model for Mission' (2002). Available from < www.globalconnections.co.uk/business.asp >.

social mobility, with new paths of opportunity opening up for achievement, status and recognition. Carey was able to achieve far more than he would have been able to had he remained a humble cobbler and Baptist pastor in the East Midlands. Developments in commercial law, such as the limited liability company, expanded and compounded this freedom. The model also provided a flexible and durable platform for co-operative action in specialized areas.

But models not only shape our thinking and practice. They also limit them and produce unforeseen consequences. No model or idea is value free and neutral. They carry within themselves certain values and ideals that influence us in unexpected ways. For example, while the 'voluntary society' model opened up opportunities for involvement in mission to a wide array of people, the business model served simultaneously to constrain and limit that involvement. The 'committee' proposed above by Carey all too easily became the expert in the task, a professional elite whose very existence (often unintentionally) marginalized and restricted mission involvement to the few. At first, the joint-stock company provided a useful way to break ecclesiastical constraints on action, and yet ultimately it created a new controlling clique. Such professionalizing trends are a recurring theme throughout the history of the modern Protestant missionary movement, as are democratizing reactions that serve to open up mission involvement from the few to the many.

Subsequent developments in corporate ideas and practice during the nineteenth and twentieth centuries had a profound impact on the operations of the mission society. The modern corporation came into being by the first part of the twentieth century, with its focus on the rationalization of production, and the application of 'scientific' principles to all aspects of management. This influenced developments in the missionary society. During the nineteenth century, women's missionary societies such as the Women's Union Missionary

Society (founded 1861) became a major feature, and by 1900 there were forty-one women's missionary organizations in America alone, which supported over 1,200 single women missionaries, and had an income of over $2 million per annum. They were so successful that they became attractive targets for 'takeover' or 'merger' by other male-led missionary societies. The arguments for this were usually based on principles of efficiency in administration and leadership. It is worth commenting that rarely did women remain in leadership in the newly merged organizations, and 'the takeover process was complete before the mid-twentieth century'.[29] The professionalization of mission was reinforced by trends in organizational development that dragged the mission agency along, whether it wanted to or not.

The apotheosis of the business approach to mission happened in 1924 with the publication of *The Business of Missions* by Cornelius Patton, one of the officers of the American Board of Commissioners for Foreign Mission. Patton wrote of his impatience with militaristic metaphors of mission, such as armies, strategies and crusades, since 'we are living in a business age, we believe as never before in business results. It is a working, rather than a fighting church to which we belong.'[30] Chapter headings such as 'Do we Mean Business?' and 'A Going Concern' serve to illustrate his theme clearly.

We see this trend continuing even more recently within mission organizations. The missionary transnational corporation (or 'international mission agency', as it is usually known) stands astride the world missionary movement like a benevolent colossus, often entering new markets (or

---

[29] Ibid., p. 14.

[30] Cornelius Patton, *The Business of Missions* (New York: Macmillan, 1924), foreword; quoted in Walls, *The Missionary Movement in Christian History*, p. 231.

'fields', as they are sometimes called) via the takeover of smaller national or regionally focused initiatives and mission agencies.[31] They are now so influential that the World Evangelical Alliance Missions Commission, until recently a network of national evangelical missionary alliances, was pressured to find a way for them to relate directly into its network, rather than through their national representatives. The 'real' transnational corporations, who comprise fifty out of the top 100 economies of the world and whose interests are now often served and promoted by national governments rather than vice versa, find their Christian doppelgangers in these organizations. This has the outcome of further 'distancing' mission from the *hoi polloi*, reinforcing the power of a professionalized elite of experts. Even if they don't act like corporations, many Western mission agencies function like the mass-membership organizations mentioned earlier.

We noted above that changing patterns of social affiliation are having a significant impact on the viability of the voluntary society. Similarly, in the past twenty years businesses have been driven to re-engineer, to downsize and to rightsize, to outsource or to consolidate, to merge and to demerge, to focus on core business or to diversify: in short, to make more changes than ever. While some of this is undoubtedly due to the growth in the number of management gurus and professors who need to make a (usually lucrative) living and reputation, it has also been driven in part by the need to respond to some of the social changes outlined in this book. Mission agencies, a blend of corporation and voluntary society, as well as being (in the UK) registered charities, have been to some extent shielded from the pressure to make changes as frequently and as quickly as

---

[31] The growth of SIM International provides a fascinating case study of this trend.

some people change their underwear. The implications of changing market conditions and social expectations take longer to filter through when a significant proportion of an organization's income comes from voluntary donations or major grants (just as it can take longer to increase these, compared to the usual business methods of increasing sales and revenue). But the social trends are now having a real impact and the pressure for change in the structure and culture of the mission agency is becoming too strong to ignore.

I would suggest therefore that the main sources of organizational stress and tension within mission agencies are not so much about the need to reorient to face new 'frontiers', but rather a result of changing socio-cultural realities that are causing fault lines and stresses within an organization.

So where do we go from here? I would suggest that a bit of daylight robbery might be the answer.

Plundering the Egyptians

The mission agency as we know it today is the hybrid offspring of the marriage of two social models: the voluntary society and the joint-stock company or business corporation. Does this invalidate its very existence, since these models can hardly be claimed as specifically and uniquely Christian or biblical? I would say not, for what other choice do we have? The only social models that we can use are those that we take from our surrounding society and culture. And this is not a particularly new approach. It is simply one of the more recent versions of a form of sanctified tomb raiding that has always been the pattern of the people of God, starting with the exodus from Egypt, the foundational event of salvation that constituted the Israelites as a people and as a nation.

Freed from servitude, the Israelites were led by Moses to Sinai, where they met with and entered into a covenant relationship with Yahweh. Once the covenant was confirmed, instructions were given for the construction of the Ark of the Covenant and the Tabernacle, whose existence was symbolic of the very presence of God among his people, a core Old Testament theological premise. Offerings of gold, silver, precious stones, fine linen and many other products were made to enable the construction of these and other artefacts of worship (Exodus 25:1–8).

But where did all these valuable items come from? For the people of Israel had until very recently been indentured workers who had been further oppressed and exploited as forced labour (Genesis 47:18–21; Exodus 1:11). In no way would they have been able to build up the reserves of wealth and valuables described above. They came instead from a combination of last-minute charitable donations and looting that took place immediately prior to the exodus from Egypt itself.

> Now the LORD said to Moses, 'I will bring one more plague on Pharaoh and Egypt. After that, he will let you go from here, and when he does, he will drive you out completely. Tell the people that men and women alike are to ask their neighbours for articles of silver and gold.' ... The Israelites did as Moses instructed and asked the Egyptians for articles of silver and gold and for clothing. The LORD made the Egyptians favourably disposed towards the people, and they gave them what they asked for; so they plundered the Egyptians (Exodus 11:1–2; 12:35–36).

This event was developed into a missiological principle by the third-century theologian Origen, whose work in Alexandria did more to relate the Christian gospel to the Greek philosophical worldview than did anyone else's. He advised his protégé Gregory[32] to study Greek philosophy firstly as a preparation for Christianity and secondly so that its ideas could be put to the service of the gospel:

> Perhaps something of this kind is prefigured in what is written in Exodus, that the children of Israel were commanded to ask from their neighbours, and those who dwelt with them, vessels of silver and gold, and clothing, in order that by spoiling the Egyptians they might have material for the preparation of the things which pertained to the service of God [i.e. the tabernacle and its artefacts].[33]

Just as we noted above that by adopting a model from business the missionary society took on features that were both expected and unexpected, so Origen was aware that 'plundering the Egyptians' could be a risky business:

> May I tell you from my experience that not many take from Egypt only the useful and go away and use it in the service of God. These are they who from their Greek studies produce heretical notions, and set them up like the golden calf in Bethel.[34]

This 'plundering' is not an isolated example. Neither the monarchy nor the Jerusalem Temple was an institution specifically commanded by God, yet they both became important vehicles for the revelation of God's truth. Nor were these structures immune from corruption, as both were criticized by the prophets for abuse and idolatry.

In the Old Testament we not only see the adoption by God's people (and by God himself) of models and structures

---

[32] Gregory Thaumaturgus, or Gregory the Wonderworker. He was a missionary in Cappadocia (and something of a miracle worker, as the attribution indicates).

[33] Origen, *Letter to Gregory*, 2.

[34] Origen, *Letter to Gregory*, 3 (in an allusion to Jeroboam, who took refuge from Solomon in Egypt and went on to set up the golden calves in Bethel and Dan – see 1 Kings 11:40; 12:28).

from the surrounding environment. We also see, from time to time, the disappearance of older structures and the emergence of new ones more appropriate for a new context. The patriarchal families disappear during captivity in Egypt, as Israel grows into an entire people, including many not of the biological line of Jacob (Exodus 12:37–38). The charismatic leaders known as 'judges' disappear with the emergence of the monarchy. And in the post-exilic diaspora, the Temple and priesthood disappear from view, and a new life of worship coalesces around the structures of synagogue and Sabbath. This pattern of adoption, transformation and replacement continues into the New Testament. Jesus himself challenged the notion of Sabbath, which had become restrictive rather than liberating. The apostles continued this trend, abandoning even the apparently divinely sanctioned practices of dietary restrictions and circumcision in the light of God's apparent work in a new era (Acts 10 – 11; 15).

The adoption of ideas and practices from the surrounding culture is not just a recurrent reality in Christian history, but also something intrinsic and valuable to the Christian faith itself. Commenting on the translation of the Christian faith from its Jewish origins, first into the Greek and Roman worlds and later into the Germanic tribal context of northern Europe, Andrew Walls comments:

> The dynamic of turning towards Christ what was already there led to an expanded process of Christian understanding … it forced people to think of the implications of daily life in terms of social identity and Christian identity, disturbing, challenging, altering the conventions of that life, *but doing so from the inside*. It was essentially a risky process, with many areas of doubt and difficulty.[35]

---

[35] Andrew Walls, 'Old Athens and New Jerusalem', *International Bulletin of Missionary Research* 21/4 (October 1997), p. 148, italics in the original. Many of the chapters in the same author's

And so, while this is risky, since 'borrowing too many things from a neighbour ... left the Western world with a very cluttered theological attic',[36] it is nonetheless essential to the very nature of the Christian faith.

At this point one might wish to point out that, in view of Origen's comment that the process of plundering the Egyptians can produce golden calves just as easily as it can produce the Tabernacle, it will be important to subject any such borrowing or spoils to a thorough theological critique. Well aware of the dangers inherent in the approach he advocated, both Origen and his North African contemporary Tertullian viewed the heresies of their day as the consequence of too close a flirtation with Greek philosophy on the part of their adversaries. Origen's advice to his pupil Gregory in this regard was to:

> diligently apply yourself to the reading of the sacred Scriptures. Apply yourself, I say. For we who read the things of God need much application, lest we should say or think anything too rashly about them.[37]

But sometimes, perhaps, the critique needs to work the other way. The professionalization of mission, whereby it is taken away from the ordinary Christian and made a matter for the expert, was an unforeseen historical consequence of the adoption of the business model by the mission agency and of the mass-membership version of the voluntary society. Its original goal and initial outcome had been to open up the possibility of missionary involvement to a wide number of people. The voluntary society has been described

---

[35] (*continued*) book *The Missionary Movement in Christian History* ably demonstrate the same theme.

[36] Harvey Conn, 'Contextual Theologies: The Problem of Agendas', *Evangelical Review of Theology* 15/3 (1989).

[37] Origen, *Letter to Gregory*, 3.

as 'one of God's theological jokes',[38] whereby a bit of judicious social plundering was used to undermine those of high theological and ecclesiastical principle whose commitment to the existing church structures and ways of working in the late eighteenth century was hindering the newly emerging missionary spirit from full expression. Sometimes it is not the 'plundered gold' that needs to be critiqued – sometimes it helps us to break us out of our encrusted and fossilized ways of thinking and acting.

Mission agencies in the new world (dis)order

Having considered the organizational models upon which the contemporary mission agency is based and the social changes that are affecting these models I have also suggested that this borrowing is not only acceptable but actually inevitable and necessary. And since these models are not working quite as well as they should be, maybe it is time to visit our neighbours again to borrow something new (borrowing being so much more socially acceptable than simply robbing them!).

> **Validity in a purely theological sense is never the only issue. To be truly suitable, mission structures must also be culturally appropriate and right for their age.**
>
> *Stanley H. Skreslet*[39]

Structures should flow from a vision for mission, and yet too often structures and institutions are directing themselves

---

[38] Walls, *The Missionary Movement in Christian History*, p. 246.
[39] Skreslet, 'Impending Transformation', p. 2.

towards preserving what we already have. The profession-alizing trends to which I have referred in this chapter serve to limit and restrict involvement in world mission. Attempts at standardization and normalization tend to have the same outcome. Playwright Bertold Brecht commented: 'the dominant viewpoint is usually the viewpoint of the dominators'. Changing patterns of social affiliation and the decline of the voluntary society create the need for new models. How can we build future-oriented structures that will serve world mission in the twenty-first century, mission that will be messy, chaotic and pluriform, yet also involve many focused, concrete and specialized stakeholders? How can we allow for diverse visions and means, facilitating mission involvement that is non-hierarchical, non-bureaucratic, personalized, immediate and local? Since postmodernity is about diversity and choice and involves a radical suspicion and critique of the nature of power, it would seem that a new family has moved in next door, providing us with the opportunity to borrow (or plunder) a whole new crock of gold.

However, before we indulge in a spate of opportunistic cat burglaries, we will look at one of the other key developments that is affecting the way that mission agencies 'do business': the rapid rise of direct action by local churches in an area previously monopolized by mission agencies.

Chapter 5

Cinderella Bites Back

The local church and world mission

World mission has been described as the Cinderella of the local church, that is, the neglected younger stepsister.[1] It is certainly true that involvement in world mission has usually been left to a small group of enthusiasts, who have sometimes through their approach and manner done their best to ensure it remains a minority interest. Basing the mission agency on the idea of the voluntary society, which by its very nature is a way of allowing those committed to a particular cause to express it in action, served only to reinforce the partition of mission from the local church.

Nonetheless, local churches have always been the mother lode from which are mined the resources that the mission agencies need, whether that be people, money or prayer. Sometimes money comes direct from wealthy individuals, but more recently the pattern has been for the 'sending church(es)' of missionaries to provide a significant proportion of the financial and other support needed.

All the signs suggest that this pattern is changing. Many local churches are becoming increasingly proactive in their world mission involvement. Not only are they wanting

---

[1] No one has ever explained to me who the two ugly sisters are. Presumably they are the worship leaders and preachers?

more of a say in the pastoral care of their missionaries, they are also beginning to set their own priorities for mission and to support only those projects and organizations that match these. And an increasing number of churches are developing their own mission projects without any reference to a mission agency at all.

These developments are, of course, not that new and have been widely commented on. They have evoked a variety of reactions from mission agencies, some positive and welcoming, and others less so, usually because they are concerned about the loss of professionalism and quality that they perceive such initiatives to represent (and obviously not for reasons of organizational self-perpetuation and the dislike of change). Even those mission agencies that are responding positively to these changes represent a journey into uncharted waters:

> Few missions executives were prepared for the rapidity of the shift from the pass-through[2] paradigm to proactive local church missions initiative. Now they are suddenly faced with a desire within many churches to partner in new ways. Many churches, in fact, are asking for training and help as they take these new steps. Frankly, agencies often are no more prepared than local churches to face these realities and may appear to be threatened by an aggressive church program.[3]

But where has this trend come from, and why should it be of such strength at this time?

As we have seen, the voluntary society provided a way for Christians committed to world evangelization to act together

---

[2] That is, a model where people and money 'pass through' a local church en-route to a mission agency.

[3] Engel and Dyrness, *Changing the Mind of Missions: Where have we Gone Wrong?*, p. 127.

in their common interest, in a way that the existing church structures of the late eighteenth and early nineteenth centuries did not. These structures, whether episcopal, presbyterian or congregational, had been argued over for centuries, and their close association with national church structures meant that few, if any, thought about what structures were needed for international action. A prevailing catholicity of spirit in the late eighteenth century may have allowed Christians of various persuasions to meet and talk together, but there was no simple mechanism available for them to act together. It has been noted that even a bishop of London found his plans for a wider missionary enterprise frustrated.[4]

So the missionary society provided a vehicle for accomplishing what local churches could not. But 'the times they are a changin'.[5] The trends highlighted in this book are manifesting themselves in, among other things, a basic distrust of institutions. One of the characteristics of postmodernity is the desire for immediacy, for involvement, for tangible and focused involvement. There is disillusion in local churches over (perceived or real) inflexibility on the part of mission agencies, over a perceived lack of accountability and over poor pastoral care. This not to say that the situation in this regard is any better inside many local churches. But the permeation of the principle of the voluntary society into local churches themselves (so that they are now little more than groups of like-minded individuals) means that they are able to organize themselves for action in areas of selected interest. And the interconnectedness and compression of the world reflected in globalization makes it easier not only to learn about situations of need, but also to respond to them without going through an intermediary such as a mission agency.

[4] Walls, *The Missionary Movement in Christian History*, pp. 243, 248–9.

[5] As noted by that eminent missiologist Bob Dylan.

Social shifts such as these have provided an opportunity for direct involvement by local churches in world mission. The drive to exploit this opportunity has come about in part through changes in ecclesiology, that branch of theology that deals with thinking about the church.

The growth in size, and more particularly in influence, of the New Churches in the UK has had a significant impact in this area. Many of those involved in the early House Church (now New Church) streams came from Brethren backgrounds, whose ecclesiology is congregational to the extreme. Even today, Brethren missionaries are usually sent out by their local assemblies, and not by a separate mission agency. Many New Churches also do the same, sometimes in association with structures associated with their stream (denomination), and sometimes not.[6] This attempt to recapture a perceived pristine New Testament understanding includes the central and unique role of the local church and casts doubt on the validity of parachurch structures such as mission agencies. The combination of theological conviction and practical action in this area has proved so powerful that churches of more conservative theological and denominational origin are now copying it.[7]

The rapid and astonishing growth of Pentecostal churches worldwide is partly based on a similar understanding of the primacy of the local church. The central place of the 'empowering of the Holy Spirit' in Pentecostal theology has meant that the call to mission is not limited to

---

[6] Work done in the 1990s by Global Connections through its Forward Together initiative and the Body International research project showed that, on the one hand, some New Churches are now working in partnership with mission agencies, and, on the other hand, that many others are involved in world mission directly, without reference even to their stream leadership.

[7] Numerous examples can be found in Tim Jeffery, *Connect!* (Carlisle: Paternoster/Spring Harvest, 2003).

a few specially trained individuals. Church planting is a fundamental principle of Pentecostal mission strategy, and the church, not the evangelist, is God's agent for evange-lism.[8] These churches are often suitably indigenized in both spirituality and in structure. In this light, their rapid growth is not surprising.

The view that the primary agent of mission is the local church (and not the mission agency) is one that commands more and more assent. It is now accepted by some as an unassailable given, and an increasing number of voices are encouraging mission agencies to re-engineer their processes and to re-position themselves not as 'agents', acting on behalf of churches in the task of world mission, but as 'consultants', expert advisors who will help local churches to fulfil their primary calling.[9] One UK mission 'agency' that exemplifies this approach, Radstock Ministries, states that world mission is 'the privilege and responsibility of local congregations rather than organisations' and believes that 'the local church is at the heart of God's mission'.[10]

Those advocating the primary role of the local church in world mission are rapidly achieving the size and status of a movement. Not everyone is yet convinced, and I include myself among the latter. My understanding of the implica-tions of globalization and postmodernity is that we are not seeing changes from one dominant way of thinking or acting to another, but from one dominant way to many different ways. So, local churches may well feature more prominently within world mission in the future than in the past, but they

---

[8]   Allan Anderson, 'Structures and Patterns in Pentecostal Mission', unpublished paper given at the Wisdom in Mission forum, Alresford, Hants, UK, 14–15 May 2002, p. 10.

[9]   See, for example, Engel and Dyrness, *Changing the Mind of Missions*, pp. 109–42.

[10] Radstock Ministries Biblical Rationale: < www.radstock. org/ who.html >.

will be just one group of 'players' among several. Globalization provides the opportunity and postmodernity provides the value system to drive both increasing involvement by local churches and also the multiplication of other ways of involvement.

What is the church? The church is the missionary people of God, sharing by faith in the promises given by God to Abraham. This includes the promise of being a blessing to all peoples and inheritor of the priestly vocation given to Israel.

So far, so good. But it is one thing to talk about 'the church' as an abstract concept. What does it mean in specific, local situations? Who gets to be included in the above definition? Are some organizational forms more central to it than others? Are mission agencies simply a temporary expedient that have no *theological* right to existence (since it is the *church* that is sent into the world in mission, rather than the church being the one who sends)? If mission agencies are not part of the church, then what are they part of?

The two structures of God's redemptive mission

Ralph Winter has given articulate expression to the case for viewing local churches and mission agencies as equal and parallel organizations within the church, viewing them both as 'redemptive structures' that can be found in existence repeatedly throughout church history.[11] Paul's pattern of evangelism ('to the Jew first, then to the Gentile') was expressed though his preaching in the diaspora Jewish synagogues of Asia Minor. This meant that the gatherings called 'churches' in the book of Acts and the New Testament letters

---

[11] Ralph D. Winter, 'The Two Structures of God's Redemptive Mission' in Winter and Hawthorne (eds), *Perspectives on the World Christian Movement*, B–45.

were basically Christian versions of the same. As such they copied the pattern of the synagogue by 'embracing the community of the faithful in any given place'.[12] This type of structure is known, says Winter, as a modality. The apostolic teams of Paul and Barnabas, Barnabas and John Mark, Paul and Timothy, and the like, represented a different structure, membership of which was based on a second additional commitment (this time to a missionary task, not simply to Christian identity and fellowship). Winter calls this second structure a sodality.

The New Testament does not define the workings and organization of either structure in clear detail, which Winter suggests is significant. It implies the adoption and adaptation of commonly understood pre-existing social patterns (in this case, both Jewish patterns of meeting and Jewish patterns of proselytization). After all, why explain in detail what everyone already knew about? The conclusion that Winter draws is that 'the New Testament is trying to show us *how to borrow effective patterns*',[13] and he proceeds to demonstrate how the twin redemptive structures of modality and sodality were expressed in later stages of church history, through the borrowing of other social patterns that fulfilled the same functions. Although he does not use the phrase, Winter is acknowledging that 'plundering the Egyptians' has been the common practice throughout the history of mission.

Thus, in the days of the early church in the Roman Empire, once the break between church and synagogue had become irrevocable and the protection that Christianity gained from being perceived as a Jewish sect had evaporated,[14] Christians sought other means of identity and

[12] Ibid., B–46.

[13] Ibid., B–47 (italics in original).

[14] As followers of a *religio licita*, Jews were excluded from participation in the Roman imperial rites. Christians were

organization. One of the earliest legal means of identity adopted by Christians was that of burial clubs, which undertook to dispose of the bodies of its members (after death, of course). Churches later began to copy the Roman civil pattern, and bishops took on the responsibility for the churches of a town or area (whereas each Jewish synagogue was independent of any other). Monasteries emerged in the fourth century AD, and many were patterned on a model developed by Pachomius, whose background in Roman military service was reflected in the communal life he developed (and which was widely copied across Europe).[15] Both church and mission structures (the diocese and the monastery respectively) developed by copying models found in the wider social context, and it was in fact the latter that provided most of the strength in medieval Christianity, and most of the help in building the former.

The rejection of monasticism by the Protestant Reformers (many of them products of the system) didn't just remove the only available instrument for missionary work for over 200 years. It also produced the continuing ambivalence within Protestant churches about separate missionary structures. The desire for church renewal by the mainstream Reformers and the restoration movements like the Anabaptists who emphasized a pure community of believers meant that the idea of a second structure for deeper commitment and involvement was viewed as anathema. The Moravian missionary movement managed to combine both church and mission structures because of their strong communal focus (bred in part by their early experience of persecution), but this case is unusual and certainly not the norm.

William Carey finally built a strong case within Protestantism for the use of separate 'means' for the 'conversion of

---

[14] (*continued*) not, and this often provided a reason for persecution.

[15] Prior to Pachomius monastic existence had largely been a solitary affair.

the heathen', using the models of the 'voluntary society' and 'trading company', even if most of the early mission societies founded in the late eighteenth and early nineteenth century were absorbed into denominational structures by the end of the nineteenth century. And so Winter views the early Protestant missionary movement of the late eighteenth and early nineteenth century, the 'faith mission' movement at the end of the nineteenth century and the later burst of new mission organizations started after the Second World War as phases in the re-emergence of the second structure (the sodality) within Protestantism, which prior to the Reformation had been a recurring feature of Christianity throughout its history.

Through this approach, first expounded in 1973 at the All-Asia Mission Consultation in Seoul, Korea, Winter argued for the formation of non-Western mission agencies in order to facilitate the missionary involvement of the rapidly growing non-Western church. Thirty years later, the non-Western missionary movement is something of a given. He has shown how the church has, at different times in its history, borrowed different models from society to organize itself, not just for local presence (modality), but also for renewal and for mission (sodality).

We have already noted that the Protestant ideal and goal of a renewed and revitalized church militates against this way of thinking, and leads to the view that the local church is the primary unit of Christian community, organization and mission. We will now examine this in more detail.

World mission as the 'privilege and responsibility' of the local church?

We are trying to answer the question of who gets to be included in the definition of the word 'church'. Winter has suggested that it should include both congregational and denominational structures on the one hand and mission agencies on the other. The common use of the terms 'church' and 'parachurch' suggest that many don't want to exclude the latter, but feel uncomfortable about including them with the former.

We will look in turn at two of the arguments advanced for considering the local church to be the primary agent in mission – the New Testament understanding and reality of the church and the place of Christian community in mission.

The New Testament understanding of the church

It is now not uncommon to hear the church of the apostolic and immediate post-apostolic era described as a missionary church, which managed to propagate itself across much of the Mediterranean world and the Middle East without the help of separate missionary structures. But how does the New Testament itself understand the church, and what do we know about the way the early church was organized?

In his article 'The Church as a Heavenly and Eschatological Entity'[16] P.T. O'Brien argues that the New Testament, while using a number of metaphors to describe the church, uses the word *ekklesia* (meaning 'assembly' or 'gathering', and often translated as 'church') in only two ways. It is either used to describe a local gathering of Christians, or it is used to refer to the heavenly and eschatological assembly of all believers in Christ. O'Brien's main argument is that the New Testament repeatedly and consistently uses the term *ekklesia* to identify visible, actual gatherings, rather than as a metaphor for God's people on earth as a whole. Thus,

---

[16] P. T. O'Brien, 'The Church as a Heavenly and Eschatological Entity' in Don Carson (ed.), *The Church in the Bible and the World* (Exeter: Paternoster, 1987), pp. 88–119.

he argues, a 'church' is a local gathering of Christians, which should be construed as 'earthly manifestations of that heavenly assembly gathered around God and Christ'.[17]

This argument is based on the wider general use of the Greek word *ekklesia* and also on its use in the Septuagint, the Greek translation of the Old Testament. From the fifth century BC onwards, the *ekklesia* was the assembly of the citizens of a Greek city state, and was regarded as existing only when assembled. Similarly, in the Old Testament, the *qahal* was the assembly of all Israel in Jerusalem, which was required three times each year. In the Septuagint, *ekklesia* is used to translate the Hebrew word *qahal*.

The outcome of this approach can be expressed as follows:

> The New Testament speaks of church in two senses. First, the church is seen as the heavenly congregation continually gathered around the throne of God. Second, it is used of local congregations which are the time and space expression of this heavenly reality. The focus of God's saving purposes for his people is, therefore, expressed in history in local congregations. The local church is at the heart of God's mission.[18]

Unfortunately, O'Brien has to resort to special pleading in certain instances to maintain this argument. References such as Acts 8:3, 9:31 and 20:17 and 1 Corinthians 4:17 and 10:32 are described by O'Brien as an 'extension' of the literal original meaning of 'gathering', to describe people who compose the gathering whether they are assembled or not. So, despite his claims, not every use of the word *ekklesia* in the New Testament refers to a literal, physical gathering – it is also used to refer to the people of God in a

---

[17] Ibid., p. 97.
[18] Radstock Ministries Biblical Rationale, paragraph 5, at < www.radstock.org/who.html >.

descriptive sense whether they meet or not. Similarly, the many references to the church as the 'body' of Christ (for example, in Ephesians 1:23; 5:23, 29 and Colossians 1:18, 24) cannot, says O'Brien, be taken to refer to all Christian believers scattered throughout the world, since he has already told us that the word *ekklesia* only means 'gathering', and obviously the whole worldwide church cannot be understood as gathering in a single place. So it must, he suggests, refer to the heavenly and eschatological assembly. The problem is that we are being asked to accept a definition of *ekklesia* taken from pre-New Testament use alone, rather than qualifying this with a consideration of how it is used in different instances throughout the New Testament. The original meaning of *ekklesia* may have been 'gathering' or 'assembly', but we just noted above that there are uses in the New Testament that show that this original sense was already being extended and used as a shorthand term for all Christian believers. So why insist that the references to the church as the body of Christ cannot be understood in a similar way?

We cannot conclude from the New Testament alone that the 'church' refers only to local congregations. A consideration of the social world of the New Testament reinforces this, and in fact leads us to see that, even in the very earliest days, Christians used and adapted models from wider society in the way that they organized themselves.

Let's begin by looking at some of the personal greetings in Paul's letters:

> Greet Priscilla and Aquila, my fellow-workers in Christ Jesus ... Greet also the church that meets at their house (Romans 16:3, 5).

> Give my greetings ... to Nympha and the church in her house (Colossians 4:15).

> To Philemon our dear friend and fellow-worker ... and to the
> church that meets in your home (Philemon 1–2).

The Roman household has been described as 'a fundamental institution of the New Testament world and of fundamental significance to the New Testament church'.[19] It was the primary social structure of the Roman Empire, a microcosm of what Augustus had made of the Empire itself. These household communities were unlike either our contemporary nuclear or extended families, and they included any number of families, usually bound together by a common agricultural or commercial enterprise and by their loyalty to the principal family of the household. It could include friends and clients as well as slaves, and was a thoroughly mixed social community. Loyalty was secured not only by commitment to the same commercial enterprise, but also by commitment to a common religion, chosen by the *paterfamilias* or household head.

In this context, we can see why the early practice of converting the head of a household was so significant (for example, Cornelius [Acts 10:1–11:48], Lydia [Acts 16:13–15] and Stephanus [1 Corinthians 1:16]). It not only led to more rapid church growth than the practice of converting individuals; it also provided a safe context within which new converts could learn and practise their faith. This also meant that it was unlikely that all the Christians in a given city met together regularly, but rather that different groups met in different houses.

So, rather than assume that the 'New Testament church' is a divinely sanctioned and unique form of organization, it is perhaps better to recognize that the earliest Christians simply organized themselves according to the patterns

---

[19] Derek Tidball, *An Introduction to the Sociology of the New Testament* (Exeter: Paternoster, 1983), p. 79.

available to them in wider society. Other considerations confirm this. We have already noted earlier that one of the first legal forms of existence taken by the church in the Roman Empire was that of a 'burial club'. A huge variety of voluntary associations, or *collegia*, proliferated in the Roman Republic and later in the Empire. They were subject to periodic ban during the first century BC because of their association with political activity and frequent outbreaks of violence. But the tendency to form associations was too strong to be resisted, and while Augustus and Claudius reaffirmed the laws suppressing them, certain types of *collegia* were still permitted. These included not only trade associations and professional guilds, but also associations dedicated to the worship of a certain god, and the above burial clubs. All such *collegia* were also able to meet regularly for social purposes, regardless of their original remit, and by adopting this model Christians were able to meet in relative security.

Nor were the missionary travels of Paul, Barnabas, Timothy and the like especially unique. Paul's work was often challenged by opponents who sowed discord among the churches he founded, and others built on his work and were viewed as his allies (Acts 18:24–27; Galatians 1:6–9; Philippians 1:15–18). The ease of travel, aided by Roman road building and the Pax Romana, meant that merchants, philosophers and wandering preachers were able to achieve their respective aims without major effort. The plethora of itinerant preachers and prophets in the late first century AD caused so many problems that rules had to be set down dictating for how long such people should be shown hospitality (Didache 11:3–6).

The New Testament does not therefore give us a pattern for 'missionary congregations' that are able to undertake mission without recourse to special structures. It has been a recurrent practice since the New Testament era for

Christians to organize themselves according to the available social models of their time. Theologically we can justify this as 'plundering the Egyptians'; historically we can justify it as a recurring pattern. William Carey's argument that 'means' are needed in order to do mission has not yet been disproved.

Mission and community

The second approach taken to emphasize the primacy of the local church in mission is to underline the relationship between Christian community and mission. This approach takes us back into the Old Testament and the role of Israel among the nations. Central to this understanding is the admonition given by Moses to Israel, just prior to their entry into and conquest of Canaan:

> Observe them [these decrees and laws] carefully, for this will show your wisdom and understanding to the nations, who will surely hear about all these decrees and say, 'Surely this great nation is a wise and understanding people.' What other nation is so great as to have their gods near them the way the LORD our God is near us whenever we pray to him? And what other nation is so great as to have such righteous decrees and laws as this body of laws I am setting before you today? (Deuteronomy 4:6–8).

Chris Wright has commented that this passage has deep missiological significance, combining ethics and mission by making Israel a model for the nations. The model of social justice enshrined in the Deuteronomic laws would cause the nations to take notice. 'The ethical quality of life of the people of God (their obedience to the law, in this context) is a vital factor in the attraction of the nations to the living God. The motivation for God's people to live by God's law is ultimately to bless the nations.'[20] And so the Christian church, it is sometimes argued, is required to embody the same paradigm. The primitive church as described in Acts 2:42–47 and 4:32–35 was exemplary in this regard. The Christian community can therefore be taken to be a primary actor in Christian mission.

But why should we accept that only local churches are to be taken to embody such Christian community? It might be reasonable to accept this if, as Ralph Winter suggested, the church 'embraced the community of the faithful in any given place'.[21] But the link between place or geography and a local church (or any other community for that matter) is now tenuous to say the least. Massive social changes such as urbanization and increased social and physical mobility mean that no longer are most of our key relationships formed in the neighbourhood in which we live. Our friendships and acquaintances are formed through work, through common leisure interests, through our children (if we have them) and, for Christians, through our churches, to which people may travel a considerable distance in order to attend.

> You chat several times a day to a stranger in South Africa, but you haven't spoken with your next-door neighbour yet this year.

We often belong to several 'communities' at once, for which the only overlapping point may be ourselves. So a local church may be simply one version of the various communities in which I live and find my identity. And these

---

[20] Chris Wright, *Deuteronomy* (NIBC; Carlisle: Paternoster, 1996), p. 49.

[21] Winter, 'The Two Structures of God's Redemptive Mission', B–46.

local churches themselves are often no less homogeneous than the other groups to which I belong.

David Bosch writes:

> In Western Protestantism the church was increasingly fractured into a great variety of denominations which were not decisively different from missionary and other religious societies. Denominations too were organised on the voluntary principle of like-minded individuals banding together [just as, we might add, are most local churches].[22]

Established state churches in Western countries (whether Anglican, Lutheran or Reformed) only create the illusion that things are different, for the existence of the many 'free' churches shows that freedom of choice exists with regard to Christian belief and practice. Tim Chester has observed that the existence of many diverse forms of Christian 'association', such as a university or workplace Christian union, a church-planting team, a diocese or denominational association, a mission agency or a Christian conference all serve to raise new questions about the marks of the church.[23] The church sure isn't what it used to be (and I don't think it ever was).

There is not much to choose between the church as bearer of mission and the mission societies.

David Bosch[24]

---

[22] Bosch, *Transforming Mission*, p. 329

[23] Tim Chester, 'Christ's Little Flock: Towards an Ecclesiology of the Cross', *Evangel* 19/1 (Spring 2001), pp. 13–21.

[24] Bosch, *Transforming Mission*, p. 329.

So we can argue that mission societies, denominational and other affiliative groups and local churches themselves are all now simply versions of the voluntary society. None can claim the monopoly on being 'the Christian community'.

I have often wondered if the longing for 'community' in our fractured, individualistic time is based on a pining for the imagined, idyllic small world of childhood. A world bounded by a few streets, our school, some friends, our parents and the parents of our friends, which evaporates forever as we journey into adulthood, when we lose contact with most of those childhood friends anyway.[25] Maybe we have romanticized 'community' into a panacea for the social ills that we see and sense of dislocation that we feel, and which we believe are caused by our fragmented urban and suburban lives. If we are Christians committed to mission, then it is easy to impute this value system on to the church, and present it as the solution to the problems of both evangelization and the 'transformation' of society. But community and mission do not always make easy bedfellows. If community is understood as the basis for effective mission, then it becomes the Holy Grail for which we search and strive. The need to build up the community all too easily absorbs our energy, leaving little or nothing left for mission. As Karl Wirth has noted:

In theory, the Anabaptist emphasis on Christian community is attractive. This line of thought suggests that as Christians meet, study, pray and live together in community, they will be equipped to bring the food of the gospel to the poor, to those who do not know God, and to the very structures of human culture ... In practice, this theory often justifies a Christian culture that understands the Christian faith as being lived out

---

[25] Hence the popularity of web sites such as < www.friends reunited.co.uk >.

primarily in Christian meetings. Since it is the community or the quality of the communal life that will witness to an unbelieving world, individual Christians direct their efforts away from relationships and action outside of the community toward participating in and increasing the quality of communal life ... The few who want to volunteer with the poor or maintain their friendships outside of the community face a constant tension: their choice to do so prevents involvement in Christian meetings that is the mark of a committed community member and growing Christian.[26]

Such a trend can be seen in the lives of the Anabaptist communities that formed during and after the Reformation. Unlike the magisterial Reformers,[27] Anabaptist[28] leaders like Menno Simons and Jacob Hutter[29] sought to establish voluntary communities of committed Christians. This concept is so familiar to many of us today that we easily underestimate how radical (and dangerous) such an approach was seen as in sixteenth-century Europe, where 'Christendom' (a situation where church and society were seen as more or less coterminous) had reigned supreme

---

[26] Karl Wirth, 'Of the Making of Many Meetings there is No End: Or, How I Learned to Stop Going to Bible Study and Love Non-Christians', *Re:Generation Quarterly* 7/2 (Summer 2001), p. 30.

[27] Luther, Calvin, Zwingli, et al, all of whom sought to bring about reformation in co-operation with the 'magistrates' (i.e. civil leaders).

[28] 'Anabaptist' means 'rebaptizer', since Anabaptists practised believers' baptism, and yet many had been baptized as infants. Most Anabaptists rejected the title, which was given to them by their opponents, and insisted that infant baptism was not true baptism. But the name stuck as a handy way of describing a large and varied number of groups who opposed the idea (and reality) of an authoritative state religion.

[29] Who gave their names, respectively, to the Mennonites and the Hutterian Brethren.

for over a thousand years. It is possible to see the early Anabaptist churches as good examples of missionary communities:

> The concept of mission was integral to such a gathered church. The Anabaptists believed themselves to be on the 'narrow' path, whereas society was on the broad path leading to destruction. They equated society with the unregenerate world, within which lived seekers after God's truth, souls who desired the strength of God's kingdom of peace. Anabaptist mission was set up to locate these seekers ... The gathered church became the base from which the call to discipleship and community was to go out through mission.[30]

The early Anabaptists were undoubtedly magnificent evangelists, travelling across Europe preaching and starting churches. The first Anabaptist church was set up near Zurich in January 1525, and the movement had expanded by 1530 to other Swiss cities, to southern Germany and Austria, and to Holland. Yet these churches ossified relatively quickly into small, introspective communities. Three reasons have been suggested for this change:

1. A loss of eschatological urgency. Many of the early Anabaptists were convinced that they were living in 'the last days'. This provided the motive for urgency in preaching, and also the resources to suffer persecution and martyrdom (which many of them did), since their suffering would not be for long. When God's final kingdom did not appear as hoped the basis for their preaching and their call to repentance and conversion was somewhat undermined!

[30] Leonard Gross, 'Sixteenth-Century Hutterian Mission' in Wilbert Shenk (ed.), *Anabaptism and Mission* (Scottdale, Pennsylvania: Herald Press, 1984), pp. 98–9.

2. After 1540, the attention of the leaders of the Anabaptist movement shifted from evangelization to the organization and maintenance of their congregations. This can be clearly seen in the topics on which even foundational leaders like Menno Simons wrote in later years.

3. Most Anabaptist communities tended to be small. This was initially forced upon them by persecution and the need to meet in secret, but even after official toleration was given the trend continued. This not only created and sustained an introspective culture; it also tended to attract only those drawn to such communities.

It is notable that the early Anabaptist successes were not due primarily to the vitality of Anabaptist communal life, but rather to their apocalyptic message and dynamic leadership. It did not come about because they were 'missionary communities'. In fact, over time, community tended to drive out mission. The missionary vitality that re-emerged among nineteenth-century American Mennonites, and which is still evident today, came not from a rediscovery of their roots but through the influence of revivalism.[31]

Community and mission may sound good in theory. In practice, it doesn't seem to work out very well.

Why here, why now?

So the theological arguments for the primary role of the local church in world mission are not necessarily that watertight. An argument based on a special New Testament understanding of 'church' is weakened by the historical

---

[31] All the above points are taken from N. van der Zijpp, 'From Anabaptist Missionary Congregation to Mennonite Seclusion' in Shenk (ed.), *Anabaptism and Mission*, pp. 119–36.

reality of earliest Christianity. An approach based on the relationship between community and mission likewise evaporates when we consider the history of this approach and the problems of defining 'community' in the early twenty-first century. But we have already noted the reality that many local churches are becoming more involved in world mission. How should we understand this? What is happening in this phenomenon?

I have already explored how I believe the two trends of globalization and postmodernity are reshaping our cultural landscape. Globalization is a handy summary word describing an increasingly interconnected world; postmodernity is at heart a radical suspicion towards power (and the institutions that wield it). Combining together, these trends are allowing for a democratization in involvement in world mission. It is not the first time that this has happened.

Many of the early missionary pioneers of the late eighteenth and early nineteenth century missionaries were of 'humble' origin, to say the least. William Carey was a cobbler, an artisan, as well as being a Baptist pastor. Robert Moffat, the father-in-law of David Livingstone, went to Bechuanaland (now on the border of modern Botswana and South Africa) with the London Missionary Society in 1816 at the age of twenty-one, having little formal education or training. He remained there for forty-eight years. Slowly, standards and expectations rose. Missionaries were required to undertake more formal training and to be of a higher educational level than hitherto. It is said that by the end of his life Robert Moffat would have been ineligible to join his own missionary society.

During the nineteenth century awareness arose of the vast unreached 'inland' areas of Africa and Asia. The high standards required by the existing missionary societies meant they did not have the people resources available to begin new work in those regions. And so a new missionary movement arose, now synonymous with organizations such as the China Inland Mission, Africa Inland Mission and the Sudan Interior Mission. These new 'faith' missions owed their origins to the holiness movement and the 1859 revivals in the UK. Intellectual ability was not despised, but what mattered was spiritual vitality. Training would be done on the 'mission field' by senior missionaries and in the cauldron of experience. The faith missions spoke of 'releasing the neglected forces of Christianity' (by which they meant the working classes and women) into the mission fields, and to a large degree they succeeded.

This pattern repeated itself in the middle of the twentieth century. Bible College training became a requirement among the faith missions, and from the 1950s onwards we see the emergence of a 'third wave' of mission organizations such as Youth With A Mission, Operation Mobilisation, Frontiers and World Horizons, all of which combine training, mission and discipleship within their programmes. Whole generations of students cut their teeth (and found themselves involved in lifelong missionary service) through involvement with these organizations.

There is a continued upwards push to professionalize within the missionary movement. By its very nature, cross-cultural mission is demanding and complex. Through bitter experience, individuals and organizations conclude that it would be better if their successors were better prepared than they were, and so the bar is raised. But mission is not, and should never be, an undertaking for a minority within the church. Mission is the church's *raison d'être*. And so it would seem to be a recurrent pattern that, as standards and expectations rise, new methods of mission involvement flow out 'from below'. What are the reasons for this? Is it the work of the Spirit of God, refusing to be limited by our ideas of what constitutes 'proper' and appropriate qualifications for mission involvement? I'm not sure I wish to be so bold as to state this unequivocally. Nonetheless, it has been a repeated characteristic of the last 200 years of Protestant missionary history, and we can view local church mission involvement (along with other major changes such as the massive increase in short-term mission) as the latest example of the same.

So what does this mean for the mission agency?

It has been a consistent theme of the last two chapters that the church organizes according to prevailing social models. The models used in the formation of mission agencies are either under threat (e.g. the declining involvement in voluntary societies generally) or are inadequate because they alienate and exclude (as we have seen by looking at the history of the business organizational model and the nature of contemporary mass-membership organizations).

Local church involvement in world mission should be seen as a good thing because it localizes and personalizes that involvement and uses an appropriate social model.

I mentioned at the end of the previous chapter that postmodernity is a new neighbour to us, one we may find it useful to visit and from whom we may 'borrow' the odd cup of sugar or an onion. And so we return to the question left hanging at the end of the last chapter. What social models does postmodernity provide for mission agencies to use?

> Today both the church and missions structures have been influenced by the values and structures of modernity. They both stand in need of new patterns of relationship … to renew their sense of missions while they make selective and wise use of the surrounding cultural influences.[32]

---

[32] Engel and Dyrness, *Changing the Mind of Missions*, p. 117.

Chapter 6

Postmodern Organizations

*Designed to thrive in a diverse
and changing world*

I don't know of any time in my 35 years of mission experience that I have seen or felt mission executives more ready and willing to change and adapt. At the same time, I also don't know of any period in my career that there is less certainty about what changes to make. The future is uncertain. We know it will be greatly different but are not sure in which ways it will be different. We know that the patterns of the past are showing 'wear' and are in need of repair. In many ways our strategies and way of thinking do not fit our present reality very well. We know that they probably won't move us into the future God has for us. Yet the new paradigms that help us interpret and organize our strategies for the future have not become clear. We seem to be in a time of parenthesis between what God has blessed in the past and what has yet to be made clear for the future.[1]

men of Issachar, who understood the times and knew what Israel should do ... (1 Chronicles 12:32).

---

[1] Paul McKaughan, President of the Evangelical Fellowship of Mission Agencies, a large network of US mission agencies, quoted in a circular e-mail.

I have lost count of the number of occasions I have heard mention of the 'men of Issachar' recently. Those 200 clan chieftains of the tribe of Issachar in ancient Israel have become a cipher for all those expressions of uncertainty about the future that characterize much of the Western missionary movement at this time. Somehow they knew what to do (in their case, it was to join David at Ziklag prior to the overthrow of Saul); if only, so the reasoning goes, we could be like them, then we too know would know what to do in our times.[2]

The longer quotation above summarizes the feelings and hopes of many in the modern Western missionary movement. It contains a clear expectation that while we live in a time of uncertainty at present at some point the contours of the new situation will become clear and we will be able to act accordingly. Eventually the whirlpool will subside and some of the bigger rocks will fall to the bottom (or the tornado will slow and drop the cows and pickup trucks to earth). The challenge is to know how to live in the interim.

But what if we are not living in an interim? What if the contemporary experience of uncertainty, diversity and complexity are not simply a transition point along the highway, but is in fact our destination, at least for the foreseeable future? What if David Bosch was correct when describing the shift from one paradigm to another?

New paradigms do not establish themselves overnight. They take decades, sometimes centuries, to develop distinctive contours. The new paradigm is therefore still emerging and it is, as yet, not clear which shape it will eventually adopt.[3]

---

[2] A literal application might suggest we should work to overthrow established power structures in favour of something new!

[3] Bosch, *Transforming Mission*, p. 349.

So it is not unreasonable to assume that, if the current period in which we are living marks such a time of change, whatever takes its place might take a little longer in coming than we may be anticipating. What if where we are now is not a waypoint but in fact the destination? We will have to learn how to live and thrive in the place in which we find ourselves, much as Jeremiah advised the first exiles from Judah after 597 BC. Denying their hopes that their state of exile would come to an early end, he wrote to them, conveying the word of the Lord:

> Build houses and settle down; plant gardens and eat what they produce. Marry and have sons and daughters; find wives for your sons and give your daughters in marriage, so that they too may have sons and daughters. Increase in number there; do not decrease. Also, seek the peace and prosperity of the city to which I have carried you into exile (Jeremiah 29:5–7).

Even if we acknowledge that the changes that are upon us will not conclude for some time, we can easily continue to behave as things were carrying on just as normal. Habits of mind are difficult to break, even if the evidence is compelling. Habits of practice are even harder to break, especially if there seem to be no viable alternatives before us.

So where do we find the wisdom that we need? From the Bible, yes, but perhaps also from our neighbours, the 'Egyptians'? And as I have suggested, postmodernity doesn't just provide us with a way of defining our current condition, but also with ideas and approaches that will help us to live and work within it. Mission agencies as they are currently constituted reflect a 200–year period of co-operation between Christianity and the cultures and worldview of modernity. As James Engel and William Dyrness have noted:

Throughout its history various movements of renewal have emerged that sought to deliver the church from its cultural captivity. In the early church and Middle Ages, monastic movements and new religious orders sought to return the church to its original mission; later the Reformation, Pietism and revivalism offered their own critiques of cultural practices that were inimical to the gospel. Notice that in every case these movements, while resisting certain cultural trends, made selective use of other cultural opportunities to organize themselves and present the gospel.[4]

The danger, of course, is that the new cultural opportunities may themselves lead to new forms of cultural captivity in the future. We have already noted the unforeseen implications of the adoption of the voluntary society in its joint-stock trading company form. We should be aware that there will be unintentional consequences of the adoption of any alternative model. But perhaps the priority for our time is to find structures and ways of working that are appropriate to the world we find ourselves in today.

> It may be possible that a niche will always exist out there for organisations that don't want to change, for executives that are willing to hang their hat on the tried and true. But if so, it's a damned small niche.
>
> *J. Huey*[5]

---

[4] Engel and Dyrness, *Changing the Mind of Missions: Where have we Gone Wrong?*, p. 116.

[5] J. Huey, *Fortune Magazine*, 23 September 1991.

So what might a postmodern mission organization look like?

It would have to deal with issues of global diversity, choice and the postmodern distrust of power, with our changing social context and shifting patterns of social affiliation, and with an expanding democratization of missionary involvement.

But such an organization could not take a single, definitive, prescriptive form (since this would go against the very ethos of postmodernity itself, which celebrates difference as an end in itself, since difference undermines dominating standpoints). A modern organization can be likened to a pendulum,[6] in that the goal is to achieve a pattern of ordered, regular activity. There is change, in that such an organization may move in one direction for a given period, only to oscillate back in the opposite direction as circumstances (like gravity) dictate. The goal of any such oscillation is to enable the system to remain in equilibrium.

A postmodern organization, however, needs a different descriptive metaphor. It is more like fire – it consumes, it flickers, it is always changing (and is remarkably hard to get hold of). Fire can't oscillate, go back over the ground it covered earlier. It is always changing, always moving on, 'all process and not much substance'.[7] The organization that sponsored the writing of this book, Oasis Trust, provides a good example of this. Even those who work for Oasis sometimes have difficulty explaining succinctly what it is and does, partly because of its variety of activities and partly because it keeps doing new things. But the nature of fire is, it keeps moving.

---

[6] As opposed to an organization that runs like clockwork, i.e. it goes round in circles.

[7] William Bergquist, *The Postmodern Organization: Mastering the Art of Irreversible Change* (San Francisco: Jossey-Bass, 1993), p. 5.

> **We are now entering a period of fire, during which old organizational forms, structures and processes will be consumed and new forms, structures and processes will emerge, like the phoenix, from the ashes of fiery consumption.**
>
> *William Bergquist*[8]

And our goal is to develop organizations that are not suited only to meet contemporary challenges, but also those that may face us in five, ten or twenty years' time, both foreseen and unforeseen.

It's not what you know, it's who you know (and what they know)

A postmodern organization is one that places a high premium on knowledge creation and conversion. One of the ways of dealing with the problems of uncertainty in both our context and in the tasks required of us is to create an environment that values experimentation, creativity and innovation (and accepts the inevitable failures that come with this). In such an organization ideas and risks are encouraged, not only because this helps us to face our immediate challenges, but also because they help to create a culture that will come up with the solutions to the problems we will face in the future (especially those that we are not even aware of yet).

We are told that we live in a knowledge economy, that knowledge is the only form of capital worth having. Unlike other forms of capital, knowledge doesn't decrease in value by being shared. Instead, it increases in value. If I have

---

[8] Ibid., p. 11.

£1,000, and give you half, then my stock of capital has gone down by 50 per cent. But if I share my knowledge with you, I have lost nothing (except perhaps the ability to charge as much money for it, since others now have that knowledge as well,[9] or perhaps the ego buzz of knowing something you don't). I don't know any less for sharing my knowledge with you. In the meantime, your knowledge has increased (so your overall stock of capital has increased in value). And it is likely that in fact my overall stock of knowledge has gone up as well, since in the interaction by which I share my knowledge with you, you will shape and add to it, thereby increasing my own understanding at the same time.

By putting knowledge in such stark terms, by describing it as a commodity that defies the normal rules of economics, we can see that the sharing of information and knowledge is not a zero-sum game (whereby one person's gain is another's loss) but a win-win situation where all parties benefit. Creating a culture where this becomes the norm isn't always easy, since most people think that 'knowledge equals power' and are often unwilling to relinquish their hold on it. But such an attitude is ultimately counter-productive, for it stifles the kind of creativity and knowledge creation that will increase the value of the knowledge held by that person. Knowledge is a dynamic product that needs to be shared and used, or it ossifies and dies. Trying to hold on to it for yourself alone will only decrease its long-term value. 'I tell you

---

9 Although even this isn't perhaps quite as simple as it seems at first sight. 'I'm paid reasonably well to write, despite the fact that I put most of my work on the Net before it can be published. But I'm paid a lot more to speak, and still more to consult, since my real value lies in something that can't be stolen from me – my point of view. A unique and passionate viewpoint is more valuable in a conversation than the one-way broadcast of words.' John Perry Barlow, 'The Next Economy of Ideas: Will Copyright Survive the Napster Bomb?', *Wired* (October 2000), p. 242.

the truth, unless a grain of wheat falls to the ground and dies, it remains only a single seed. But if it dies, it produces many seeds' (John 12:24).

> **Computers store information; people know things**

One of the easiest mistakes to make when thinking about knowledge creation and conversion is to assume that it is primarily about information and communication technology. If you begin by thinking in terms of databases, information capture, Intranets and the like, then you have started in the wrong place. Knowledge is not the same as data or information. Knowledge is not an object or a commodity. It cannot be easily stored in the freezer until needed and it has a fairly short expiry date if it isn't used. It doesn't exist apart from the people who hold that knowledge in their heads and hearts.

For knowledge has a 'social life', that is, it needs to get out and about, meet people, mingle and network. We should think in terms of 'communities of practice', small groups of people who have a common bond that cuts across organizational boundaries. They share common values and mutual respect. They have been described as 'a group of people who are informally bound to one another by exposure to a common class of problem'[10] and are key to the implementation of successful knowledge creation. Until new ideas are embedded in these groups, it is safe to assume that no real learning has taken place. And yet they can also

---

[10] Brook Manville, Director of Knowledge Management at McKinsey & Co. Consultants, quoted in Jeremy Hope and Tony Hope, *Competing in the Third Wave* (Boston, Massachusetts: Harvard Business School Press, 1997), p. 79.

be the key places within which knowledge is shared and applied to new problems. The challenge is to work out ways for this knowledge to be taken and applied within other communities of practice, since each community has boundaries of culture and expectation, which can be difficult to overcome, especially as they are so often unarticulated and invisible. But given that the missionary movement claims to have some expertise in cross-cultural communication and living, these shouldn't be insurmountable barriers.

> **Don't mistake the edge of your rut for the horizon**

This concept of 'communities of practice' helps us to identify the different types of knowledge sharing that we might want to be involved in. Conversations and research in areas that are broadly similar to our own are the most likely to be of immediate relevance. Because we are interacting with people whose interests are akin to ours, assumptions and values are often fairly similar. But knowledge creation isn't just about the sharing of information. It is also about taking insights from one discipline or area and using them to resolve problems in another. This is a key outworking of the concept of 'plundering the Egyptians' – taking something of value from one context and using it elsewhere to create something valuable. I personally find it much more interesting to read 'off the course' than to follow the set texts and in doing so often discover insights that can be applied fruitfully to the issue at hand. My hope is that this book will be an example of the value of this. And so we need to meet with and learn from those who are very different from ourselves and whose concerns and foci are different. This is always risky, since it is possible that there will be little common ground, and so we will pass by one another like ships in the night. But it is also potentially very fruitful, as it can lead to the generation of new knowledge and insight that would not otherwise have been available.

> I milk a lot of cows, but I churn my own butter.

I would like to use the example of Global Connections to illustrate the implications of these ideas. We can see its numerous groups and forums as examples of the 'communities of practice' in action. There are over twenty such forums in operation, divided into three discrete groups: regional (where the focus is on a given region of the world, such as Africa, Latin America, etc.); functional (where participation is based on fulfilling a given function within an organization – personnel, short-term programme co-ordinators, youth workers, etc.); and ministry, where a common ministry focus (healthcare, relief and development, missionary kids and the like) provides the glue that holds the group together. Since participation in these groups is open to all 150 plus mission agencies that are members of Global Connections, each one cuts across organizational boundaries and provides a helpful forum wherein its members can meet others working in a similar field, discuss common problems and issues and also to plan for joint action to resolve these.

Since each forum has its own 'customer base' (few organizations that work in Africa send people to the Latin America forum), cross-fertilization across groups is somewhat limited. It happens to the extent that personnel officers from organizations working in those respective regions can share knowledge within their own 'community of practice' and so take back useful information to apply within their own region, but given that their common concern would be personnel issues, their discourse would tend to be restricted around this core. With the desire to facilitate the kind of interdisciplinary conversations and learning that I mentioned above and that are both potentially irrelevant but also potentially highly productive, I proposed and saw through the implementation of a 'new-style' conference for the whole Global Connections network. This conference brought together all twenty plus forums in the same place at the same time, for forty-eight hours of input, discussion, sharing and learning around a common issue. We provided focused learning opportunities with sessions for each forum, and also for interdisciplinary learning through the use of 'matrix groups', to which people were allocated. These matrix groups combined people from different organizations, which worked in different regions of the world, and who had different roles within their organizations. It was risky, since most or all the groups could have failed to connect. I was very relieved to find out that most people found the matrix groups a great success.

In the context of the above considerations, information and communication technology has a useful place. Provided it facilitates human interaction and doesn't become a *simulacrum* of it, ICT can support the generation and conversion of useful knowledge. But it doesn't do it by itself. People have to get involved with one another.

So the first characteristic of a postmodern organization is that it places a high premium on the value of knowledge creation and develops a culture in which this is facilitated. Only by doing so can it be prepared for the uncertainties of the present and the future.

Low walls around the garden

An organization can be said to be 'postmodern', and thereby fitted to thrive in such a context, by the extent to which it takes seriously the postmodern distrust of power and celebration of difference as well as the weakening patterns of social affiliation characteristic of postmodernity. And yet by definition an organization seems best equipped to do the opposite. Most organizations (and mission agencies are good examples of this) work on the basis of conformity and commitment. How can an organization exist, never mind succeed, unless there is a clear understanding of who is in and who is out and what it is trying to achieve?

These two features define all organizations, including mission agencies. They have a reason for existence (a mission or purpose) and operate under a specific set of rules or norms (boundaries). This twofold definition provides us with a useful way to understand the distinctive nature of a postmodern organization.[11]

A premodern organization usually has unclear boundaries (with little distinction being made between work and family life) and an unclear mission (other than the provision of food and shelter for the family). By contrast, a modern organization has very clear boundaries. Just as modernity itself drew a sharp distinction between the public and private spheres, so the modern workplace draws similar lines between the workplace and the home. The factory gate is a good example of a place where such a line is drawn. But it is not characterized by a clear sense of mission other than the need to make a profit. Mergers and acquisitions can be undertaken with relative ease (even if the long-term viability of such actions often proves elusive). The large conglomerate provides a classic example of such an organization. In many

---

[11] This concept is taken from and forms the main content in Bergquist, *The Postmodern Organization*.

ways, the modern missionary society reflected these values. Mission agencies were able to begin new work in diverse 'fields' that had little or nothing in common with each other, provided the 'bottom line' (i.e. income and personnel levels) didn't prevent it. The goal may not have been to make a profit, but the same factors constrained or permitted decision making.

A postmodern organization reverses these features. The drawing of boundaries incensed many postmodern writers, who pointed out that such boundaries were often arbitrary and always an exercise of power. Keeping boundaries open or blurred helps to resist the selective use of power and also assists in the democratization of mission that the increasing involvement of local churches and the growth in demand for short-term mission programmes both represent.

But how does one maintain any kind of direction in such a situation? Open boundaries leave an organization vulnerable to many and powerful competing demands on its time, energy and attention. It resists them by having a clear sense of mission, one that is widely owned and understood by all its stakeholders.

> **Without a clear sense of purpose and values, organisations can splinter or become aimless vagabonds or scavengers that feed destructively on other organisations and segments of society.**
>
> *William Bergquist*[12]

A clear sense of vision and purpose is vital in our plural, diverse context. In *Thriving on Chaos* business guru Tom Peters argues that:

---

[12] Ibid., p. 67.

being unique – standing out from the growing crowd of competitors, products and services – is an essential for survival. Such uniqueness must be understood and lived by everyone in the organisation. While niche-market-oriented, higher-value-added strategies are increasingly the winning hand, low-cost producers can [also] be successful.[13] On the other hand, an 'in-between' or 'stuck-in-the-middle' – i.e. not unique – strategy is unfailingly disastrous.[14]

One example of the 'unclear boundaries, clear mission' concept in action is the food court of a shopping mall. Several different food providers all compete therein for your custom. It is not uncommon to see KFC, Burger King, Pizza Hut and other franchises side by side, each selling a clearly defined and distinct product. But the seating area is common to all: no single food provider has the monopoly on any part of this. The mission of each is clear but, within the context of the food court, the boundaries between them are meaningless. Each and every franchise is open to the person who frequents the place.

You can also buy a postmodern 'people carrier' in the Ford Galaxy, Volkswagen Sharan and Seat Alhambra. Externally almost identical, apart from its badge and name, the customer is invited to make a distinction based on the brand values ascribed to each of the vehicle makers. The boundaries between the three vehicles is so unclear as to be almost non-existent, yet each manufacturer has a clear sense of its own mission and values as expressed in its brand.

Mission agencies tend to have fairly high boundaries. Their membership categories make it very clear who is 'in'

---

[13] Examples such as Wal-Mart, EasyJet and Dell illustrate this maxim.

[14] Tom Peters, *Thriving on Chaos* (London/New York: Harper-Collins, 1987), p. 166.

and who is 'out'. Most local churches are excluded by these boundaries, and only those individuals that are willing to surmount the high walls are welcomed as insiders (all too often being separated in some way from their churches in the process). Yet these boundaries may not be necessary, since most mission agencies have a clear sense of mission (either in terms of ministry or geographical focus). Reducing their membership or partnership boundaries would allow them to involve more churches and more individuals at a variety of different levels of integration. Retaining their clear sense of mission (and ensuring that this was widely owned and understood by all concerned) will help to reduce the danger of being dragged in a thousand different directions at once, or having the central vision become so diluted as to be almost meaningless.

Our faltering attempts at partnership between mission agencies in the UK have not got us much further than the 'food court' approach described above (and even then I think we sometimes get all 'proprietary' about the 'seating arrangements'). Africa Inland Mission Europe's Associate Director, Mark Forshaw, comments: 'Personally I think that for many of us, partnership is having our display stands together. But is that unity of effective action?'[15]

Can we even begin to think about producing the missionary equivalent of the Ford Galaxy/Volkswagen Sharan/Seat Alhambra? Persistent (and so far unsuccessful) attempts to create a central administrative and donor-management function that would serve a number of mission agencies have foundered on the rocks that guard the organizational boundaries of mission agencies, despite continual hard work by Stanley Davies of Global Connections and a number of gifted and committed associates to try to create such a service.

---

[15] Mark Forshaw, personal e-mail, 15 November 2002.

For an organization to develop a vision that will allow it to live with unclear boundaries, this vision needs to be a shared one, and commonly owned. The process of creating this will change, shape and develop the vision. As new actors join the organizational orbit the vision will be further adapted and shaped. So a key question to be asked is, 'How adaptive and diverse should an organization become?' For, on the one hand, if our current context of continual change and diversity is likely to continue, then 'leaders of organisations in the postmodern world must repeatedly re-examine organisational purposes and values, for the world is constantly changing and demanding new and different products and services'.[16] On the other hand, small organizations can also be effective, not by diversifying but by focus and specialization, 'gap-filling' in the areas left by larger organizations.

This interplay between clear mission and responsiveness can be explored by thinking of the vision as an 'anchor' to provide stability in a confusing, rapidly changing environment. But while this helps us to avoid being swept along by a powerful short-term trend, can any organization be indifferent to changing tides and currents (sticking with our nautical theme)? If turbulence and unpredictability are our long-term context, is an anchor really that helpful? We are probably most familiar with the concept of a ground anchor, which we usually see hanging from the bow of a ship, and which is dropped in shallow water to hold a ship in a given place. But this is no use in deep water or where the bottom is unstable. Here, a 'sea anchor' is used. A tapering cone, thus slowing the passage of water through it, the sea anchor stabilizes the movement of a ship, helping it to survive in turbulent or critical conditions. It also gives us a viable metaphor for understanding the balance between

---

[16] Bergquist, *The Postmodern Organization*, p. 67.

stability of vision and flexibility of response needed in a postmodern organization.

Regardless of the decisions taken in the areas of diversification or focus, and clear direction or responsiveness, organizations suited to a diverse postmodern context will be flexible with regard to their boundaries, establishing market niches, shifting with the changing market, all the while preserving a specific identity and purpose. And while we may not feel comfortable using these concepts, the market that mission agencies are in is definitely shifting. It may not be easy to define who the customer is and who is the supplier for a mission agency (the UK local church, the overseas community or church, etc.), but few would deny that in all respects their market is changing. The challenge for leaders of postmodern organizations is that 'they must know their market and what business they are in'.[17]

Radstock Ministries provides a good example of the kind of mission agency that embodies the principle of 'stability of vision and responsiveness to changing circumstances' as well as the 'clear mission, unclear boundaries' principle. Growing out of Friedenstimme UK, which focused on helping the persecuted church of Eastern Europe, the fall of communism in the late 1980s presented the organization with a key decision – should they retain their focus on helping persecuted Christians, but in other parts of the world, or should they retain their existing geographical focus, but change the kinds of ministry they were involved in to suit the new circumstances? They chose the latter course, and today continue to focus their attention on Eastern Europe, the Baltic States, Russia, Ukraine and the rest of the former Soviet Union. What makes them a good example of the 'clear mission, unclear boundaries' principle is that from the early 1990s they decided to prioritize the direct involvement of local churches in mission in their area of interest,

[17] Ibid., p. 77.

for which they undertake a facilitating role. This is a central value for all of Radstock Ministries' work. Those who work for the organization largely act as co-ordinators of the work of those churches in a given region. Are these churches working as part of Radstock Ministries? No, they are undertaking their own mission work. Yet their work is supported and co-ordinated through Radstock, and so they are in some way associated with the organization. So we can see that the 'edges' of Radstock Ministries are fuzzy, even blurred. It is impossible to quantify exactly what the work of the organization includes. But their clear vision that world mission is the 'privilege and responsibility' of the local church provides coherence and direction in a complex and changing environment.[18]

Postmodern leadership: juggling cats in a sandstorm

The role of leaders merits special attention. Diverse, unbounded organizations need a distinct style of leadership. The leaders of the modern era worked within ordered, bounded organizations. As such they often had to be good managers, able to develop structures and processes that would allow their organization to fulfil its goals. They provided guidance and training, continuity and planning.

William Bergquist suggests that the postmodern leader, by contrast, is more like a butterfly.[19] The full implications of this statement can be seen if we consider this simile in terms of chaos theory. In this context, 'chaos' should not be taken to imply the kind of open, random, indeterminate and confusing reality that we usually associate with the term 'chaotic'. Instead, it refers to a third state, located between

[18] For more information about Radstock Ministries, visit < www. radstock.org >.
[19] Bergquist, *The Postmodern Organization*, p. 95.

such 'open random' systems and 'closed' systems (which provide the classic Newtonian image of nature as a determinate system, a perfectly constructed watch that functions with regularity and order according to its maker's instructions). 'Chaos' is an 'open self-organizing' system, which betrays evidence of order even though there is clearly no external organizing agent acting upon the system. Order is provided internally by the system through what are sometimes called 'strange attractors'. Examples of this include Mandelbrot patterns, crop circles, sand dunes, snowdrifts and the like. It has also been likened to a liquid state, which exhibits ripples, waves and eddies, unlike both gases (the 'open random' system) and solids (the 'closed' system).

One of the least understood but most significant sayings in relation to chaos theory is the expression that 'a butterfly flaps its wings in China and causes a tornado in America'. Notwithstanding the meteorological improbability of such a phenomenon, it expresses clearly the idea that in a chaotic system a small event that occurs in a specific time and place can have a profound impact in a much wider sphere. This usually happens, according to chaos theory, when the system is pushed across a 'bifurcation point' into a new order of being. An example of this would be an avalanche. The potential for such an avalanche builds up slowly, as snows falls and drifts. At some point, a relatively small action triggers an avalanche (a loud noise, or perhaps just that final snowflake that is 'the straw that breaks the camel's back'), and huge changes follow.

Small actions and events have much more impact on a chaotic system than on a solid system (glaciers rarely turn into avalanches), and since postmodernity can be likened to a liquid[20] (and hence chaotic) state, so likewise the small

---

[20] E.g. Zygmunt Bauman, *Liquid Modernity* (Cambridge: Polity Press, 2000).

actions of a leader can have a large impact. But the outcomes of such changes are highly unpredictable, since chaotic systems are highly sensitive to initial conditions (no two avalanches are ever alike, or, to take a more mundane example, the marbles in the children's game Kerplunk never fall in the same way twice), and can have an effect way beyond what can be predicted, controlled, or even desired.

In such a context being a butterfly is a risky business. Who knows what kind of small actions will lead to enormous messes that someone has to clear up? OK, that's a fairly pessimistic view of the possibilities for change offered to a butterfly by a chaotic system. But it does mean that leadership in a diverse, chaotic context is going to be less like that envisaged by Thomas Carlyle – 'No great man lives in vain. The history of the world is but the biography of great men' – and more like that proposed by Charles Handy, 'Great visions from great people ... are in short supply at the "end of history". It is up to us to light our own small fires in the darkness.'[21] 'Change comes from small initiatives which work, initiatives which, when imitated, become the fashion.'[22] And William Bergquist, 'Postmodern conditions usually require small steps towards renewal rather than elaborate plans.'[23]

Like a butterfly, postmodern leadership has a limited time in which to live (or make an impact). It must constantly change directions with the wind, and it is not protected like the chrysalis. Like the organizations they lead, postmodern leaders have to be very clear about their mission and purpose, all the while fluttering in a turbulent environment and accepting that some outcomes may be the exact opposite of what was foreseen or intended. Moments of glory are

---

[21] Charles Handy, *The Empty Raincoat* (New York: Random House, 1995).

[22] Ibid.

[23] Bergquist, *The Postmodern Organization*, p. 14.

often brief and unseen. I find it hard to conceive of a clearer parallel to the concept of servant leadership so often enjoined on Christians.

This servant role can be extended further. In an organization with blurred boundaries leaders have to spend a lot of time on integration and collaboration, ensuring that the vision is commonly owned, understood and acted upon. They act as the 'glue' for the organization, through the creation of a sense of community and belonging, and as the servant of those with whom they work. Old-style command-and-control approaches have to be replaced by ones based on partnership and co-operation, where mediation and negotiation skills are at a premium.

Creating mission agencies fit to face a diverse and changing future

Postmodernity can be described as '*vive la différance*'. Any organization that wishes to thrive in a changing context needs to encourage the exploration of difference so that the knowledge creation abilities needed to respond to unforeseen future events will be developed and available when needed. It needs low or unclear boundaries to allow those who represent this difference to be able to connect to and participate in the organization. It simultaneously needs a clear and widely owned understanding of its mission and purpose to provide direction amid the chaos. Leadership in such organizations has an integrative role, seeking to identify those differences that really do make a difference (a particular challenge, given that modern approaches to leadership, because of the emphasis on standards, structures and processes, tend to encourage and reward non-difference).

In the next chapter, we will look at an organizational structure that might help to fulfil these requirements – the network.

Chapter 7

'Let's do Lunch'

The network as the organization of the future

Al-Qaeda is multinational, with members in numerous countries and a worldwide presence. Senior leaders in the organization are also senior leaders in other terrorist organizations, such as the Egyptian al-Gama'at al-Islamiyya and al-Jihad. Al-Qaeda seeks a global radicalization of existing Islamic groups and the creation of radical Islamic groups where none exist.

It supports Muslim fighters in Afghanistan, Bosnia, Chechnya, Tajikistan, Somalia, Yemen and Kosovo. It also trains terrorist organizations from such diverse countries as the Philippines, Algeria and Eritrea.

Al-Qaeda's goal is to 'unite all Muslims and to establish a government which follows the rule of the Caliphs'. Bin Laden has stated that the only way to establish the Caliphate is by force. Al-Qaeda's goal, therefore, is to overthrow nearly all Muslim governments, which are viewed as corrupt, to drive Western influence from those countries, and eventually to abolish state boundaries.

Al-Qaeda may have several thousand members and associates. It also serves as a focal point or umbrella organization for a worldwide network that includes many Sunni Islamic extremist groups, some members of al-Gama'at al-Islamiyya, the Islamic Movement of Uzbekistan, and the Harakat ul-Mujahidin.

It has cells worldwide and is reinforced by its ties to Sunni extremist networks. Coalition attacks on Afghanistan since October 2001 have dismantled the Taliban – Al-Qaeda's protectors – and led to the capture, death or dispersal of Al-Qaeda operatives. That said, the organization still survives, is still active, and is still a threat.[1]

It might seem a little odd to begin a chapter in a book on the future of Christian mission agencies by looking at one of the most widely reviled (and, in some circles, most widely fêted) terrorist organizations of the early twenty-first century.

The reason for selecting this example is that, despite the incredibly ferocious assaults on Al-Qaeda and the Taliban regime in Afghanistan after the atrocities committed in the USA on 11 September 2001, Al-Qaeda survives. It remains, in the eyes of the US Department of Defense, an active threat. The Taliban government in Afghanistan – a more conventional organization that was by definition restricted to a particular location – has been destroyed. Al-Qaeda has lost much of its co-ordinating and training capacity but, as recent tapes issued by the organization (which may or may not be from Osama Bin Laden) show, it has lost none of its power to motivate. While some of its continued vitality is no doubt due to the passion and commitment of its members, it is also due to the way it structures itself. Al-Qaeda has remained a potent threat because it is a loose network of like-minded people and organizations.

---

[1] Composite summary taken from US Department of Defense Background Briefing on the Al Qaeda Terrorist Network, 19 February 2002 < www.fas.org/irp/world/para/alqaeda_dod 021902.html >, 'Patterns of Global Terrorism 2001', US Department of State, May 2002 < library.nps.navy.mil/home/ tgp/qaida.htm > and the Federation of American Scientists Intelligence Resource Program < www.fas.org/irp/world/para/ ladin.htm >.

The network structure has underpinned a number of other successful organizations recently. The International Campaign to Ban Landmines, which along with its co-ordinator Jody Williams was awarded the 1997 Nobel Peace Prize, and the Jubilee 2000 Coalition, which persuaded several governments to write off debts owed by Third World countries, are two such examples. All three of the organizations mentioned above have benefited from a network structure that allows passionate and committed individuals and groups to contribute to a wider purpose (whether for good or ill) with a minimum of co-ordination and administration. Widely seen as an effective antidote to bureaucracy (the corporate equivalent of arthritis), the network has arrived as the organizational structure for a globalizing postmodern world.

Surfing the Third Wave

When you're in the business of selling the future, it's easy to make great claims. It's also good business. Frighten the natives with some well-chosen predictions that play on their paranoia, package it up in a best-selling book and lucrative business seminar, and laugh all the way to the bank. Yet not all futurists can be safely accused of this. One of the most widely respected, Alvin Toffler, has had such an impact that the titles of the two books for which he is best known, *Future Shock* and *The Third Wave*, have entered common parlance, and are familiar even to those who have never heard of the author or who didn't even know that they were book titles. What singles Toffler out from the rest of the seers and soothsayers is that, although his books were written some twenty-five years ago, many of the trends he identified have actually come to pass. For example, we noted earlier in this book the trend towards personalized scale and mass-customization in most parts of our lives today. In 1980, Toffler wrote the following:

> The hidden code of Second Wave society encouraged a steam-roller standardization of many things – from values, weights, distances, sizes, time, and currencies to products and prices. Second Wave businessmen [sic] worked hard to make every widget identical, and some still do. Today's savviest business-men, as we have seen, know how to customize (as opposed to standardize) at lowest cost, and find ingenious ways of applying the latest technology to the individualization of products and services.[2]

Toffler's thesis in *The Third Wave* is that there have been three great social transformations in human history (enu-merated, perhaps unsurprisingly, as the First, Second and Third Waves). These waves mark breakpoints in history; key times of discontinuity that lead to the dawning of new eras. Prior to the First Wave, human society was structured in its most primitive form. *Small groups* of hunter-gathers co-existed alongside one another. Overall, population numbers were small, groups were little bigger than family sized, and often they were migratory. The First Wave is marked by the development of agriculture, which allowed the first human settlements to emerge. The first cities appeared in the Ancient Near East and the structure of human society changed. It could now be categorized by *hierarchy*, with a small aristocracy and priesthood ruling over a larger peasant population, although some pre-First Wave societies survived among nomadic and small tribal groups. Toffler's Second Wave coincides with the Industrial Revolution in Europe in the eighteenth century. Enlighten-ment thinking encouraged the application of rational

---

[2] Alvin Toffler, *The Third Wave* (London: Pan, 1981), p. 265.

principles to human society in an attempt to order it more efficiently. *Bureaucracy* thus became the archetypal organizational principle of the post-Second Wave world. Toffler argues that the Third Wave has been breaking upon us since the end of the Second World War. Characterized variously as the Information Age, a post-industrial era, the era of disorganized capitalism, or, as I have suggested, by globalizing postmodern diversity, the Third Wave is taking us into a new period in human history. And the organizational form that is best suited to this diverse and complex situation is the *network*.

So what is so special about a network? Why should it be so appropriate for a complex and diverse time such as ours?

Networks are OK with diversity

The first great strength of networks is that they can cope with variety and complexity. Instead of requiring standard operating principles across an entire organization for the sake of consistency, networks are by nature diverse. In a postmodern context that is suspicious of all attempts to define a norm, this is both welcome and appropriate. One thing we should note about the different organizational forms identified above is that the emergence of a new form doesn't mean the extinction of what came before. The *small group* might be the most 'primitive' form of social organization, but that doesn't mean they don't exist any more. Quite the contrary. We noted earlier in this book that the small group has not gone away and it is still a highly appropriate organizational form for our time. Reporting on contemporary Argentinian protest movements and the local assemblies that have sprung up in many districts in an attempt to reclaim some sort of local autonomy, social activist and author Naomi Klein comments: 'in an age of global networks, it is the small-scale and the local that have the greatest strength'.[3] Similarly, *hierarchical structures* exist in any organization that is too big for everyone to know everyone, or where there is simply a need to agree on who gets to make the decisions and who gets to execute them. *Bureaucracy* still fulfils a useful function in bringing order to complex tasks. It can manage much more complicated situations than can a small group or hierarchy (where everything gets decided 'at the top'). But bureaucratic structures also reach the point where change and uncertainty outrun its ability to keep up, hence the need for network structures. But these networks contain all the preceding organizational forms: they don't do away with them, they just change the context they exist in.

The global anti-capitalist movement is a good example of the kind of network that embraces an array of participating groups and organizations, many of which might in other contexts be opposed to one another. During the protests at the World Trade Organization meetings in Seattle in 1999, environmental groups both small and large (like Greenpeace) combined with anti-capitalist anarchists and blue-collar American unions to effectively hijack the agenda of those meetings. The variety of organizations involved, diverse in size, focus and agenda, did not prevent their effective co-operation towards a mutual goal.

Networks are about connections

Networks can embrace a wide variety of stakeholders, and so they develop a second great strength. Because there is less need to focus attention on making sure that each member or 'node' of the network fits into a coherent predetermined pattern, more time and energy can be spent on the links

[3] Naomi Klein, 'Out of the Ordinary', *The Guardian* Weekend Magazine, 25 January 2003, p. 22.

between these nodes. What matters are the connections; what is connected is much less critical. The key to an effective network is the communication between its various parts, and, as we have noted, interaction between groups that are different from each other is a prerequisite for the kind of knowledge creation that is required to thrive in an ever-changing and complex environment.

> **Live in fragments no longer. Only connect.**
>
> *E.M. Forster*[4]

The value of linkages has been demonstrated in a variety of different settings, from the American Revolution through the value of e-commerce firms to dealing with drug abuse.

Paul Revere's midnight dash around the towns and villages of eighteenth-century Massachusetts and his cry 'The British are coming!' is as well known to every American as Churchill's 'We will fight them on the beaches' is to every Briton.[5] Having been alerted to plans by the British to march on the provincial towns of Lexington and Concord, in order to arrest the colonial leaders John Hancock and Samuel Adams and to seize the guns and ammunition stored by the colonial militia in those places, Revere rode through the night to forewarn the local communities. Within five hours, word had reached Andover, forty miles to the west of Boston. By the following day, the colonial militia had assembled at Concord and defeated the British army in a skirmish that marked the start of the American Revolution.

[4] E.M. Forster, *Howards End* (Harmondsworth: Penguin, 2000), ch. 22.

[5] The fact that we know less about Revere in the UK is probably because most of us tend to focus on the wars that we won!

What is less well known about these events is that Revere's friend William Dawes undertook a similar ride at the same time, heading in a different direction, and yet few men from the towns he rode through fought at Concord. In *The Tipping Point*[6] Malcolm Gladwell suggests there was a good reason why Revere succeeded where Dawes failed. Revere was what Gladwell calls a 'connector'. He was gregarious, sociable and active in local politics in Boston. He acted as a link between the various 'committees of correspondence' that sprung up in colonial New England in protest against the 1773 Tea Act (which led directly to the now-famous Boston Tea Party). During his night-time ride, Revere knew whose doors to knock on. Dawes didn't. The linkages and connections made the difference.

The ridiculous over-valuing of the now-infamous 'dot.com' businesses in the late 1990s made (and lost) many a fortune. What is less recognized is that since the bursting of the dot.com bubble in autumn 2000 e-commerce firms may now be valued at more realistic levels, but their share prices are still on average higher than comparable 'bricks and mortar' businesses with similar incomes and earning potential. Research done at Duke University, North Carolina, has shown that the number of visitors to a web site, the number of members of an online community (even commercial ones like eBay), the quantity and variety of member-generated content and the accumulation of data about visitor preferences all combine to produce 'network advantages' which are reflected in future business performance:

> The stock market continues to value network advantages stemming from traffic even after the April 2000 crash in Internet stocks. Network advantages created by web traffic are positively associated with analysts' consensus forecasts of one-year

[6] Malcolm Gladwell, *The Tipping Point* (London: Little, Brown, 2000), pp. 30–34, 56–9.

and two-year ahead earnings. In particular, network advantages appear to increase future sales more than future expenses.[7]

Systems thinking stresses the fundamental interconnectedness of the parts of any system, so that they cannot be treated in isolation from one another. This is in stark contrast to a reductionist approach that seeks to isolate the various elements of a system and 'fix' the problem areas. The interconnectedness inherent in large, complex systems means that simple actions produce large, unintended outcomes. An example of a non-system approach to the 'drug problem' would be to cut off the supply to the streets. In a reductionist sense, the problem is thus solved. In reality, what happens is that dealers then resort to raising prices and 'cutting' the doses with other chemicals, causing addicts to steal more to feed their habit and to run even worse health risks.[8] Problem solved?

Time and again the value of thinking in terms of linkages and connections can be demonstrated. And a network is the best organizational form to ensure that such links are strong and effective.

Networks are adaptable

As well as being able to include an assortment of stakeholders and provide the means for them to link with one

---

[7] S. Rajgopal, M. Venkatachalam and S. Kotha, 'The Value-Relevance of Network Advantages: The Case of E-commerce Firms', *Journal of Accounting Research* (December 2002). Available at < www.faculty.fuqua.duke.edu/~rajgopal/bio/files/JAR%202002b.pdf >.

[8] Simon Caulkin, 'Thinking Outside the Box', *The Observer*, 26 May 2002. Available at < www.observer.co.uk/business/story/0,6903,722116,00.html >.

another, networks have another advantage in a world of unpredictable change – they are flexible and adaptable. Taken as a whole, and especially if it contains a wide variety of different types of member, a network can adapt to almost any sort of change. It can be likened to a flotilla rather than a supertanker. If it is heading towards rocks in a storm, the supertanker is too cumbersome to turn and avoid the oncoming disaster. Some of the flotilla might also be lost in the same situation, but most will survive. The persistence of the Al-Qaeda network in the face of unrelenting pressure is a case in point.

> [It] is a blueprint of how Bin Laden currently operates, using a loosely tied network of local militant groups that operate with his blessing and support, but which cannot be easily traced directly back to him. It is also this loose structure that makes it so difficult for intelligence and police agencies to disrupt the network.
>
> A former Egyptian militant described the structure of radical Islamic groups as having been modelled after 'a bunch of grapes'. 'Each group operates independently with its members not knowing who the others are. That way, if one member of the group is plucked off by police, the others remain unaffected,' he said.[9]

On this occasion, we would wish that the organization concerned had not learned to make use of the advantages that a network structure confers. But it serves to illustrate the lesson nonetheless.

The Internet provides another good example of the flexibility of a network. It was originally created to ensure that US

---

[9] Richard Engel, 'Inside Al-Qaeda: A Window into the World of Militant Islam and the Afghan Alumni' (2001). Available at < www.janes.com/security/international_security/news/misc/janes010928_1_n.shtml >.

government and military communications could continue in the event of a nuclear attack. Messages are broken down into 'packets' and distributed along the communications links that exist and then reconstituted into a single message at the receiver's end. The efficacy of this system was demonstrated on 11 September 2001 in the aftermath of the terrorist outrages at the World Trade Center in New York. Telephone systems were unable to work (mainly because many of the lines and mobile telephony antennas had been destroyed along with the Twin Towers). But e-mail continued to work, as the communications systems simply worked around the parts of the network that no longer functioned.

So there are three main reasons why networks function so well in a globalizing postmodern world. They can include great variety, they allow a focus on linkages (with all that means for knowledge creation) and they are flexible, able to cope with uncertain and changing conditions.

We noted earlier in this book the observation that since missions structures are based on the appropriation of organizational forms existing in wider use they are subject to the same weaknesses that beset their secular counterparts. I'm not claiming that networks are a panacea, but that they are probably the best structural type for our present time. What are the weaknesses associated with a network?

It's not all beer and skittles

Motivated by a desire to do away with all types of control and direction, it can sometimes be assumed that networks 'just happen', and that they work best when left to themselves, without any central co-ordination. Advocates of such an approach tend to use the Internet as a model of the kind of network they envisage:

The Internet has no central control. It has no headquarters; no force masterminding its development; no institution running it. It consists of lots of computers and the links between them. The links are not organised in any hierarchical or centralised network. They are self-organising. Contributors to the network create these links in an *ad hoc* way.[10]

In many ways this is a valid description. The Internet is a network that is open to all (or to all who can afford the computers to access it and who have the education and technical skills to produce web sites – so not quite *all*). But it also takes a slightly romantic view of the Internet as something that *just happens*. But this is not the whole story. Some of the assertions in the above quotation are not the case in reality. The World Wide Web Consortium (or W3C, as it is sometimes known) is an organization that includes most of the main stakeholders of the global Internet community, many of them the corporations such as Microsoft and Cisco, that provide the hardware and software that makes the Internet run. The W3C was formed in 1994 to ensure the development of common protocols that could be applied to the whole of the Internet. This is why a web site designed for one browser (such as Explorer) can be viewed in other browsers (such as Navigator and Opera). The W3C's existence and effectiveness can be seen in the fact that we are encouraged to design web sites to HTML 4 standards (someone had to define what those standards were, and why 4 is better than 3, 2 or 1). Its self-description is as follows:

W3C's mission is to lead the Web to its full potential, which it does by developing technologies (specifications, guidelines, software, and tools) that will create a forum for information,

---

[10] Chester, 'Christ's Little Flock, p. 20.

commerce, inspiration, independent thought, and collective understanding.[11]

There's nothing sinister about the W3C. There's no *éminence grise* lurking in the background to your experience of the web, deciding what you can and cannot view (unless you live in China or have protection software like Net-Nanny installed). The W3C works at all times to ensure that wide access, trust and innovation remain at the heart of the Internet's development.

So even the Internet isn't really a network that just happens, as if by magic. This fact is further illustrated by the ubiquity of search engines (when did you last try looking for a web site by just typing in a URL, hoping it might be right, and successfully find what you were looking for?). The title of Master of the Universe of search engines currently belongs to Google, which logs the content of and provides access to over 3 billion web pages. Google has a distinctive 'page-ranking' system that prioritizes pages according to how many other web pages link to it. So it operates as a kind of 'peer review' system. When you search for a subject using Google the pages listed first are those that most other web pages think deal with the subject you are looking for. There's no single human mastermind deciding who gets listed where (and in cyberspace, if you're not listed by a search engine, or more realistically in the first two pages of results, you don't exist). It's a neat solution to a complex problem (which is why Google has been so successful).

So even the most anarchic network needs some facilitation. And like all facilitation, it isn't without its problems. Google is a case in point. In one case, it was forced to remove a link to a Norwegian anti-Scientologist web site. The site included (without permission) excerpts from

---

[11] < www.w3.org/Consortium/Points/ >.

Scientologist publications. Using the US Digital Millennium Copyright Act 2001 (which limits Internet piracy) the Church of Scientology threatened to sue Google unless it complied with their request to remove the site from its listings. In another case, the government of China threatened to restrict access to Google by Chinese web site users unless it removed links to web sites about, for example, the Falun Gong, Taiwan and Tibet. The Chinese government is notorious for its Internet censorship (it is common to speak of the Great Firewall of China). Again, Google caved in (to the dismay of those free-speech advocates who regard the Internet as their own special domain).

And it's not just virtual networks that need good, impartial facilitation.

We noted earlier that Al-Qaeda has retained some of its potency despite the destruction of its central communications and training facilities. It may not be toothless, but it has nonetheless had its claws trimmed. The US Department of Defense press briefing about Al-Qaeda in February 2002, quoted at the start of the chapter, made the following observations:

> It's changed ... [We took] away its primary safe haven, which was Afghanistan, it was the one place it could do basically all the business it wanted to do in one safe, controlled spot ... it had freedom of action, freedom of training, freedom of movement, freedom to meet ... al Qaeda has lost ... its center of gravity. It's lost its safe haven and its common meeting place. The benefits of Afghanistan cannot be underestimated ... it's been disrupted ... and we believe that the leadership is probably going to go more decentralized. It's going to be more of a franchise-type thing.[12]

---

[12] US Department of Defense Background Briefing on the Al Qaeda Terrorist Network, 19 February 2002. Available at < www.fas.org/irp/world/para/alqaeda_dod021902.html >.

So Al-Qaeda remains a threat. But without its co-ordinating hub it is (thankfully) less effective than it was.

A centralized co-ordinating function is not simply something that can be imposed upon a random network. But it has been demonstrated in a number of contexts that, sometimes without intending that such a function should exist, it emerges anyway. It appears to be a feature of networks that a co-ordinating and facilitating hub is a prerequisite for effectiveness, and if one doesn't exist it will materialize anyway.

Michael Schrage uses the example of airport hubs. While large airlines such as American Airlines and British Airways have long been committed to a 'hub-and-spoke' network typology, where the vast majority of flights feed into a few key airports, lower-cost competitors such as Southwest Airlines developed an alternative point-to-point structure. Yet Southwest's success has seen its own flight densities increase at key airports such as San Jose, Oakland and Las Vegas. It has inadvertently created its own network hubs, without really meaning to. If networks don't design their own hubs, they evolve anyway. Schrage suggests that the critical hubs – 'the O'Hares and the Heathrows' – dominate the creation or destruction of network value.[13]

Another example of the critical importance of the 'hub' to the successful operation of a network is seen in the now-famous 'six degrees of separation' test devised by Stanley Milgram in the late 1960s. He wanted to test the veracity or otherwise of the idea that any two people on earth are separated by no more than five other people connected to each other in some meaningful way.

Milgram tested the idea in the following way. He got the names and addresses of 160 people in Omaha, Nebraska, and sent each of them a packet. On this packet was the

[13] Michael Schrage, 'Network Theory's New Math', *Strategy+ Business Magazine* (fourth quarter 2002). Available at < www. strategy-business.com/press/article/?art=9966476&pg=0 >.

name and address of a stockbroker who lived in Sharon, Massachusetts, and who worked in Boston. Milgram asked each person to send the packet not to the stockbroker but to a friend or acquaintance that they thought might be able to get the packet closer to the stockbroker in order that it might be hand-delivered. The recipient was then to try to do the same. And so on. So the first recipient might, for example, send the packet to someone they knew in New England, not because they would know the stockbroker in question, but because they would be more likely to know someone else who might. On each occasion, the recipient was asked to write their name and address on the packet, and, once the packets were delivered to the stockbroker, Milgram would be able to tell how many people had played a part in ensuring each packet's arrival.

What Milgram found was that most packets were delivered to the stockbroker after passing through only five or six people's hands. This fact in itself is surprising, but what is more remarkable is the role played by a few key individuals in the delivery of most of those packets to the stockbroker. Twenty-four packets were delivered to the stockbroker's home, sixteen by the same person. All the remaining packets were delivered by two different people to the stockbroker's office. In all, notwithstanding the varied and idiosyncratic ways that 160 people sent out those packets, half were delivered by the same three people. Malcolm Gladwell, who relates this story, comments:

> Six degrees of separation doesn't mean that everyone is linked to everyone else in just six steps. It means that a very small number of people are linked to everyone else in a few steps, and the rest of us are linked to the world through those special few.[14]

---

[14] Gladwell, *The Tipping Point*, p. 37.

It was no accident that the 1997 Nobel Peace Prize (mentioned earlier) was awarded jointly to both the International Campaign to Ban Landmines and to its co-ordinator Jody Williams. Such 'connectors' are the network hubs. Without them, networks don't (work, that is).

Another weakness of networks is that they are not good at charting a single course. Returning to our earlier nautical analogy, networks are not like single supertankers, nor are they like a military fleet. They are like a flotilla that has agreed to go to a certain place, but not necessarily in the same type of boat, or by going the same way. Networks can include many competing interests, even among those committed to a common cause. One executive of the engineering giant ABB, which has a federal/network structure, commented that 'sometimes all you can do is watch the herd, and observe with relief that, in general, they seem to be heading in the right direction'.[15] I was very aware during my time at Global Connections that we had very little power to change what its member organizations did, though we did have a degree of influence which often surprised me and which called for careful judgement.

On balance, even if some of the weaker members of the herd fall by the wayside, networks are able to adapt well to changing conditions and to thrive in them. The weaknesses we've looked at don't invalidate the network concept, but they do mean that networks are not perfect – but they are probably the best structure for our time.

Networks: real world examples

It is one thing to be part of a network and to draw on the benefits that such participation confers. But it is a different

---

[15] Handy, *The Empty Raincoat*.

thing again for an organization to structure and operate as a network in itself. How have some organizations involved in world mission worked this out in practice?

Global Connections

From 1996–2002 I worked as Associate Director of Global Connections, the UK evangelical network for world mission. It was known as the Evangelical Missionary Alliance (EMA) when I joined the organization, and as part of the process of re-launching it as Global Connections I applied some of the above understanding of what a network is and does to our structure and operations.

A review of the organization's image and strategy conducted in 1998–1999 confirmed what we had already perceived, which was that the UK missionary movement was (contrary to popular opinion) not in a state of free fall decline. Instead, it was healthy and growing. Granted, some mission agencies were working hard just to maintain their current income and activity (and, in some cases, failing to achieve those goals). Others were more successful in this area, seeing steady growth. What we also noticed was that new forms of mission involvement were developing, new charities that were unlike the older missionary societies were being formed, and local churches were taking a more proactive approach to their own missionary work, sometimes without any reference to a mission agency at all. The outcome could be summarized as a diversification of the stakeholders involved in world mission in the UK.

As EMA, we faced a choice at that time. We were perceived to be primarily associated with the older, more traditional, missionary societies (although this perception did not entirely correspond with reality, as EMA had long been helping new organizations and local churches to develop their own global mission activity). We could decide to stay focused on our existing constituency/customer base, or we could expand our perceived remit to include all newer forms of mission involvement as well. We chose the latter course, consciously naming ourselves as a network (hence the strapline 'the UK evangelical network for world mission'). At the time, I described our intention as being to 'combine the wisdom and expertise of the past with the creativity and innovation of the present'. We wanted to ensure that all those included in the network were able to learn and benefit from the strengths of others. This was to be done so that older organizations did not simply continue their slow descent and the newer actors were able to draw on the expertise that did exist (and of which they were often unaware). As such, we became a more diverse network, able to include different types of organization, not just those that fitted a specific pattern. New 'Associates' schemes were launched to allow churches and businesses to link more easily into the network (prior to this no effective mechanism had existed to allow these groups to participate in EMA/Global Connections activities, at least since the decline of Interaction[16] in the early 1990s).

Having resolved the problem of allowing diverse stakeholders into the network, we looked in more depth at how the connections between network members could be improved. We had to develop a strategy to facilitate network-wide learning. This strategy consisted of two elements.

The first element was to increase the emphasis on the various groups and forums operated by Global Connections. The number of groups and forums was expanded to over twenty, so that members of the diverse network could meet with those who had similar concerns for mutual support and

---

[16] Interaction was the name for an EMA scheme to help local churches (it began life as the 'Fellowship of Church Missionary Committees' in the mid 1980s and was given the snappier name a few years later).

joint action. The forums became the primary entry-point for most people into the Global Connections' network.

The second element was the development of a web site that would make available the knowledge and insight shared within those groups, as well as conferences and other forums. The Internet has enabled the development of new technologies that make relevant information available 'just in time' (rather than 'just in case') for those who want to go looking for it. With over 200 papers available for download from the Global Connections web site at the present time, there is no way that all that knowledge and learning could be sent to everyone within the network just in case they might find it useful. By making it available online, it was nonetheless available in an accessible format, not hidden away in some filing cabinet or stored on a hard drive somewhere.

Global Connections is also well able to adapt to any future changes that affect the UK missionary movement. By being a network for all stakeholders, it can continue its work regardless of the future shape of the sector as a whole. Its expertise in partnership and co-operation and its ability to facilitate networking and knowledge creation will remain available regardless of the overall shape and balance of its varied and diverse membership.

Mennonite Mission Network

The Mennonite Mission Network is the mission agency of the Mennonite Church USA. That denomination was formed in 2002 through the union of two American denominations, the General Conference Mennonite Church and the Mennonite Church, both based in the mid-Western USA. The Mennonite Mission Network came into being as a result of the merger of two denominational mission agencies, the Commission on Overseas Mission and the

Mennonite Board of Missions, as well as one denomination's Commission on Home Ministries. Its purpose is to facilitate the mission outreach of the Mennonite Church's congregations, both in the USA and elsewhere.

As its name indicates, the Mennonite Mission Network has consciously conceived and structured itself not as a single organization but as a network. For that reason, it prefers not be known by its acronym MMN, but by its full name, or as the 'Network'. Executive Director Stanley Green comments:

> We are seeking to create a new understanding of a mission agency
> – one that supports the overall mission capacity of all parts of the
> church, rather than a central institution that performs mission on
> behalf of the church. Acronyms are institutional. The name
> signals our intent that the Mennonite Mission Network build a
> resource network throughout the church that will equip congregations and all parts of the church to do God's mission.[17]

In his earlier role as President of the Mennonite Board of Missions (MBM), Green had reflected that MBM had to:

> anticipate a radical transformation of the organizational system
> and its image. We needed to adapt our self-identity from that
> of a centralized bureaucracy that 'owned' the mission (we
> designed the initiatives, deployed the personnel, and then
> courted and cajoled congregations to support our program) to a
> more decentralized, networking entity focused on developing
> synergistic partnerships with regional Mennonite conferences,
> congregations, and international partners.[18]

---

[17] Mennonite Mission Network FAQs, available at < www. mennonitemission.net/aboutus/faqs >.

[18] Stanley W. Green, 'How Mennonites Repositioned a Traditional Mission', *International Bulletin of Missionary Research* 23/4 (October 1999), p. 162.

As a network, the Mennonite Mission Network is conscious that this allows it to include a more varied and broad constituency within its activities:

> A mission board can convey the impression that decisions are made in an autocratic fashion by a small group of people sitting around a table. A mission network, by contrast, can incorporate many different people who choose to work together because they have a similar vision for a specific ministry.[19]

The self-understanding of the Mennonite Mission Network also reflects the idea outlined earlier that a network is more concerned about its linkages than the entities so linked:

> Our congregations, conferences, seminaries and denominational offices are the many parts of the body, each with its vital function in carrying out God's mission. At the Mennonite Mission Network, we see our function as the circulation system, ensuring that God's mission flows to all parts of the church.[20]

The Mennonite Mission Network is also aware that the structure it has adopted allows it to be very flexible in the light of unforeseen contingencies, as the following excerpts from a consultation held during the Network's change process makes clear:

> Choosing a particular organizational model is less critical than being positioned for continual change. We must design functions and structures in order to be able to change quickly and responsively.
>
> Twenty-first century mission must be organized for continuous change and learning. Placing mission workers at the

---

[19] Mennonite Mission Network FAQs, available at < www.mennonitemission.net/aboutus/faqs >.
[20] Ibid.

frontiers of mission can lead to organic and inclusive operations. Collaboration between individuals and agencies must be fluid, evolving as learning takes place. The result will be mission programs that are responsive, open-ended and dynamic.[21]

Serving in Mission/SIM International

SIM began life as the Sudan Interior Mission in 1893. It has grown considerably in recent years through mergers with other mission agencies. SIM has have recently restructured to enable the organization to fulfil its goals more effectively. It has adopted a federal structure, which, while not a network in name, uses in practice some of the principles of a network we have identified above.[22]

The SIM federation is defined as 'a community of villages united by common vision, purpose and overall policies'. These villages include the functions normally described as 'sending offices' and 'field/ministry teams' and are defined as 'local communities empowered to take innovative action within the framework of the federation'. The inclusiveness displayed by a network is implicit in this definition, and it is made more explicit in SIM's intention to 'adapt procedures and systems to allow involvement in SIM from a wider constituency'. This is possible to the extent that standardized expectations are relaxed, allowing those who are different from the norm to feel included and a full part of the federation.

---

[21] 'Emerging Trends in North American Mission Agencies – An External Perspective', Mission Study Task Group II, Mission Transformation Project Team, Mennonite Church USA, October 2000, pp. 6, 8.

[22] The information about SIM International, including all quotations, is taken from a presentation given by Malcolm McGregor, SIM UK Director, at the Wisdom in Mission forum, Alresford, Hants, UK, on 14–15 May 2002.

There is a strong emphasis on knowledge creation and innovation being facilitated by the federal structure. Directors of the sending villages are expected to work closely with one another to stimulate creative ideas in recruitment, PR and church relations. An Advisory Services Group exists to support the sending and ministry villages, and its role is to network widely and stimulate visionary action.

We also noted earlier that a network works best when it has functioning hubs. The International Administration of SIM has a clearly defined role in the federal structure. While it holds the villages accountable, its primary role is not to direct but to encourage and support the activity of the villages, to stimulate networking between them and to co-ordinate the use of people and finances. Even this co-ordination is not absolute. Sending villages now have the freedom to work directly with ministry villages/fields, rather than channelling all their activity through an international co-ordination function. Within this structure, the sharing and co-ordination of knowledge is important, as is the management of the linkages. This is a primary purpose of the Advisory Services and International Administration functions.

SIM has not become a network to the same extent as our previous example, the Mennonite Mission Network. But we can see that the federal model SIM has adopted uses the network principles identified earlier to introduce the kind of flexibility that an ever-changing globalizing postmodern context will require.

A final thought: in praise of serendipity

I have argued through this chapter that networks are a useful structure for the kind of context we have been looking at in this book because they are inclusive of difference and more able to adapt to continual change. A strong emphasis on linkage and connection creates the conditions for the kind of knowledge creation and innovation needed in a changing environment. We have also noted that networks need hubs in order to function effectively.

But what a hub must not do is to try to co-ordinate and manage all the activity that goes on within the network. Applying the principles of rational management in order to optimize efficiency is what makes bureaucracy good at managing some complexity but hopeless at managing too much of it.

Networks are good at producing serendipitous events, those accidental happenings that prove to be very beneficial. And, by their very nature, they can't be planned. Mathematicians Duncan Watts and Steve Strogatz found that when a few random connections were introduced into a small network the network became more efficient and more effective. They create small worlds from great complexities, improving the overall performance of the system rather than ruining it. In short, random links allow new and useful hubs (like Gladwell's 'connectors' mentioned earlier) to emerge.

Watts and Strogatz' theories have been applied to the structure of proteins, food webs in an ecosystem, the grammar and structure of language and to the architecture of the Internet. Intel and Motorola found that using randomness to link circuits on their semiconductors made them run faster and more efficiently. Michael Schrage comments that:

> engineers are now aggressively exploring the role of randomness in performance enhancement of their products. Purely rational design that once treated randomness as the enemy has been transformed; designers now play with randomness as a tool to create 'small worlds' that exploit this power of serendipitous connection.[23]

---

[23] Schrage, 'Network Theory's New Math'.

The moral: hubs are important, but they must not try too hard to organize a network. Their role is to create the conditions for the network to 'do its stuff'.

Chapter 8

Midget Gems, Wolves and Lambs

Making diversity work

When I was young one of the things I liked to do was to go down to the local corner shop with my friends to spend some of our pocket money on sweets. If I was a bit short on cash, then 'a quarter of Midget Gems'[1] featured fairly frequently in my purchasing decisions. Midget Gems were great, because (a) they were cheap, (b) they were small so you got a lot of them and (c) they came in a variety of different shapes, colours and flavours. The various chemically induced flavours not only gave us an unnatural high that would today be handled with a course of Ritalin; they also provided us with an early introduction to the principles of the market economy and the laws of supply and demand. The off-white/clear ones, ostensibly grapefruit flavoured, were both the most popular and the fewest in number (and so could be traded for two or even three yellow or orange ones), whereas the pseudo-liquorice black ones couldn't be given away. Nonetheless, the mixture was part of the attraction.

The theme of this book has been that, because of the huge changes embodied in the terms 'globalization' and

[1] 4oz, or about 100g. The web site < www.aquarterof.co.uk > takes advantage of the nostalgia for childhood sweets (and you can get Midget Gems from them!).

'postmodernity', diversity and choice are increasing in all areas of life. Postcolonial theories of culture help us to recognize that differences also exist within cultures, not just between them. We have also looked at how the mission agency has changed and how it now faces a new set of changes if it is to remain effective and even justify its very existence. This includes developing ways of working that can include difference, rather than trying to reduce or remove it. We have looked at how postmodern organizational structures like the network might provide ways of doing this.

Mission agencies are encountering increasing problems with diversity. The large and diverse non-Western missionary movement has helped to bring to the fore the challenge of integrating different national and ethnic cultures in many mission organizations and contexts. More recently, awareness has been increasing of different generational cultures and the 'problem' of retaining Generation X missionaries.

Turning a problem into an opportunity

Rather than simply being a problem to be managed or reduced, this diversity can be a resource that brings advantage. It is not just a reality; it is also an asset.

Early attempts at diversity management formulated it in moral terms. It was seen as something that was ethically 'right' to do, even if it took time to achieve and wasn't as effective as working with homogeneous teams. Common cultural assumptions are a strong bonding mechanism, and it was long assumed that organizations and teams that were built on a common base would be more able to 'cut to the chase', and so would become more productive and higher performing quicker. Diversity was seen as a moral luxury.

Each culture makes its own assumptions as to how individuals think and learn, can be influenced, may be changed, or might be motivated ... But what works in one culture will not work, or not work so well, in another. Cultural harmony is health as well as happiness ... The first essential of organisational efficiency is cultural purity. To each his own god. Harmony is health. It is when the gods compete within one activity that confusion results.[2]

More recently, it has become recognized that diversity can contribute to the performance of an organization or team. In situations of continual change and environmental uncertainty, contexts that encourage rather than suppress difference are more likely to generate the creativity that comes up with innovative solutions to unforeseen challenges.

Existing intellectual capital is not enough. New ideas and knowledge must be created to generate internal breakthroughs in how the business operates and external breakthroughs in finding and working with new partners. A workforce with diverse perspectives provides a rich resource for creativity.

New ideas will not be enough for success. It requires the inventiveness and resourcefulness of all employees to transform intellectual capital and ideas into viable products and solutions. Where will this inventiveness come from? From a diverse workforce whose contrasting perspectives can generate a competitive edge.[3]

Such diversity can also help us to become more aware of our own cultural preconditioning. It is easy to assume that our preferred way of doing something is the best or only way.

[2] Charles Handy, *Gods of Management: The Changing Work of Organisations* (London: Arrow, 1995), pp. 46, 68.
[3] Interview with Terence Brake of TMA Americas, available at < www.dialogin.com >, 11 March 2003.

Multicultural teams have a built-in, heightened sensitivity as to what is biblical and what is cultural about themselves. They help their members to see themselves and the host culture from outside their individual cultures. Diverse cultural backgrounds provide perspective and help the team, as a unit, to respond appropriately.[4]

Name Six Famous Belgians

The biggest problem facing this line of argument is that an acceptance of difference doesn't 'just happen'. In fact the opposite usually seems to be the case. People seek out and feel most comfortable with those who are most similar to them. 'Birds of a feather flock together' is an old saying that illustrates how much this seems to be a fact of human nature. People prefer the familiar to the unfamiliar.

In his short story 'Name Six Famous Belgians'[5] David Slavitt illustrates this preference with a story about Harry and Joan, an American couple spending a holiday visiting various cultural sites in Sicily, southern Italy and Rome. Their goal was to find 'a certain degree of insulation from the abrasions of life'. Yet Harry and Joan's hotel in Palermo offered free insurance to its guests, in case they were victims of theft or worse. They attempt to laugh this off until a young teenage bag-snatcher tries to make off with Joan's bag.

---

[4] David Greenlee, Yong Joong Cho and Abraham Thulare, 'The Potential and Pitfalls of Multicultural Mission Teams' in Kelly O'Donnell (ed.), *Doing Member Care Well: Perspectives and Practices from around the World* (Pasadena, California: William Carey Library, 2002), p. 400.

[5] David Slavitt, 'Name Six Famous Belgians' in David Slavitt, *Short Stories are not Real Life* (Baton Rouge, Louisiana: Louisiana State University Press, 1991), pp. 43–57.

They later make friends with an English couple called
Paul and Dotty, who tell them of a game played by some of
their colleagues whenever they drive across Belgium en route
to the Frankfurt Book Fair (Dotty works in publishing).
The game is called 'Name Six Famous Belgians', and, as
Paul notes, 'the wonderful thing is, it can't be done'.
Harry's response to the idea of this game is indicative of his
increasing dislike of Italy and the Italians: 'Maybe that's a
good thing, though, I mean, that it's so tough. I like the idea
of ordinary people leading ordinary lives. Famous people
are frequently villains.'

Harry and Joan's experience of Italy goes from bad to
worse, until they pitch up in Naples, trying to find somewhere to eat. As it happens, at the very same time Italy is
playing football against South Korea in Mexico City during
the 1986 World Cup finals. When Italy wins[6] the whole of
Naples erupts into a frenzy of celebration, with cars and
scooters careering recklessly around the city, horns blaring,
drivers and passengers cheering and celebrating.

> The street, which had been quiet a moment before, was alive
> with people now, swarming with traffic, loud, blaring, grating,
> triumphant, frenzied, insisting on the wonderfulness of their
> being Italians, their national pride and ebullience bubbling up
> and spewing forth.

This assault on their sensibilities is too much for Harry and
Joan, and within days they are at home in Philadelphia. And
where did they tell their friends that they had spent their
entire holiday? Belgium.

---

[6] Unlike in the same match played sixteen years later in Seoul,
South Korea.

Lord of the jungle

A dislike of that which is different might strike us as normal human behaviour. But it would seem that God intends something else:

> The wolf will live with the lamb,
>> the leopard will lie down with the goat,
>> the calf and the lion and the yearling together;
>> and a little child will lead them.
> The cow will feed with the bear,
>> their young will lie down together,
>> and the lion will eat straw like the ox.
>
> The infant will play near the hole of the cobra,
>> and the young child put his hand in the viper's nest.
>
> They will neither harm nor destroy
>> on all my holy mountain,
>> for the earth will be full of the knowledge of the LORD
>> as the waters cover the sea.
>
> (Isaiah 11:6–9)

Now Isaiah's vision of the 'peaceful realm' doesn't correspond too closely to current reality. There are not too many problems when the lambs are kept together in a field. Nor does keeping the wolves in a pack cause too much disruption. However, putting the two together is a recipe for chaos and bloodshed. Practically speaking, it might seem as though the best thing to do with people that are different is to keep them separate, to segment, to specialize. This can seem particularly wise when you want to help to develop things that would otherwise be dominated or destroyed by others. The best way to raise a healthy flock of sheep is not to give the shepherding job to a wolf.

As a white, Anglo-Saxon, English-speaking male, I am aware that in most situations of (for example) multicultural diversity I am in the position of the wolf. Men tend to dominate over women. My natural facility with my mother tongue (which by a sheer accident of historical hegemony has become the lingua franca of most international meetings) gives me an advantage in communication in such contexts. I am halfway through completing what I am saying before others have even had time to formulate a contribution into what is their second, third or fourth language. On top of this, other less-recognized cultural forces come into play.

An emphasis on different national or ethnic cultures, some of which behave as 'wolves' while others take on the role of the 'lamb', has featured strongly in the work of Geert Hofstede. Starting in 1966, he undertook a major research project in a single multinational corporation, IBM. In the course of the project, employees of IBM located in fifty different countries completed some 116,000 questionnaires. From this research, Hofstede was able to identify different characteristics of national cultures, looking at, for instance, the degree to which they emphasize the individual or the group, their degree of tolerance of ambiguity and their focus on achievement and success or the care of others. He also identified cultures according to their 'power distance', that is, the degree of inequality in a society and the extent to which this is accepted. In 'high power distance' cultures, hierarchy is accepted as normal, and everyone has their rightful place. Superiors and subordinates have their respective roles and tend not to mix. The powerless do not feel as though they can change the system, although they may try to ascend the power hierarchy to their own personal benefit, after which, of course, they will have no incentive to change the order of things. Major changes can usually only happen when the powerless combine to overthrow the established elite, through revolution, and this usually results in the formation of a new power elite.

> **They knew how to be errand boy and clerk, and I knew how to be boss.**
>
> *Ilyas Halil*[7]

'High power distance' countries tend to be found in the non-Western world, although Hofstede also included 'Latin' and other southern European countries, such as Portugal, Spain, Greece, Yugoslavia, France and Belgium in this group. An illustration of the differences in power found in such contexts and the limited ability of the powerless to change the status quo even as they strike back at the powerful is illustrated in Gabriel García Márquez' story 'One of these Days', in which a poor, small-town dentist 'without a degree' is visited by the Mayor, who is suffering terrible toothache. The dentist tells him that he will only be able to remove the tooth without anaethesia as the Mayor has an abscess. As he removes the tooth, the dentist says, 'Now you'll pay for our twenty dead men.' The treatment over, the Mayor tells the dentist to send the bill. 'To you or to the town?' replies the dentist. The Mayor didn't look at him. He closed the door and said through the screen: 'It's the same damn thing.'[8]

'Low power distance' cultures, by contrast, are those in which people believe that inequality should be minimized. Hierarchy may be acceptable to the extent that it allows

---

[7] Ilyas Halil, 'No One to Yell At' in Ilyas Halil, *Unregulated Chicken Butts and Other Stories* (Salt Lake City, Utah: University of Utah Press, 1990), p. 37.

[8] Gabriel García Márquez, 'One of these Days' in Gabriel García Márquez, *No One Writes to the Colonel and Other Stories*, J. S. Bernstein (tr.) (London: Harper & Row, 1968), pp. 109–10.

different tasks to be accomplished in an organization, but that is all. Superiors and subordinates should treat each other as equals, with equal rights. Those with power should try to look less powerful than they actually are. Education is widely seen as an acceptable route to gaining more power. Countries with 'low power distance cultures' include Anglo-Saxon, Scandinavian and other northern European nations, such as the UK, the USA, Canada, Australia, Ireland, Germany, Sweden and Norway.

In international or multicultural contexts, people from 'high power distance' cultures tend to act as though they are powerless, whereas those from 'low power distance' cultures behave as though they have power. The result? The latter (usually Westerners) dominate the discussions and the planning, whereas the former appear to sit back and let them. The wolves take over; the lambs get out the way before they are devoured.

We have already noted the postmodern desire to identify and challenge the use of power. Hofstede's high/low power distance concept helps us to focus on this as an important issue in any context of diversity. How can we encourage the kind of diversity that allows Isaiah's vision of the wolf and the lamb 'lying down together' to be experienced as reality?

Children of the revolution

First-century Palestine belongs to those cultures categorized as 'high power distance'. And Jesus spoke some powerful and revolutionary words into that context:

> Blessed are you who are poor,
>   for yours is the kingdom of God.
> Blessed are you who hunger now,
>   for you will be satisfied.

Blessed are you who weep now,
    for you will laugh.
Blessed are you when men hate you,
    when they exclude and insult you and reject your name as evil,
    because of the Son of Man.

Rejoice in that day and leap for joy, because great is your reward in heaven. For that is how their fathers treated the prophets.

But woe to you who are rich,
    for you have already received your comfort.
Woe to you who are well fed now,
    for you will go hungry.
Woe to you who laugh now,
    for you will mourn and weep.
Woe to you when all men speak well of you,
    for that is how their fathers treated the false prophets.

(Luke 6:20–26)

Eric Law, a Chinese–American Episcopalian priest, says the following about this promised revolutionary change in the order of things:

In the Judeo-Christian tradition, the attitude towards the powerful and rich is very different from the attitude toward the poor and the powerless. The powerful are challenged to give up their power and wealth, and redistribute it in order to achieve equality among the people of God. To the powerful, the emphasis is on serving and being humble.

The powerless, however, are lifted up, cared for and loved by God because of their faithfulness. God has compassion on those who are oppressed and suffering. They are loved by God even though they have no worldly power. They are blessed even though they are suffering now.[9]

Law suggests that 'power analysis' is a vital skill to be developed and applied in any context of diversity. The Bible has a lot to say about God's intervention on behalf of the powerless. Yet Christians rarely find it easy to identify with, for example, Pharaoh's army as it chases after the escaping Israelites, or with the proud Pharisee who proclaims his own righteousness, compared to that of the abased tax collector. This is perhaps not surprising, since it doesn't take long in reading these stories to see whose side God is on, and naturally we want to be on that side.

I was once working with a church youth group on a weekend away, and I was taking them through some of the things Jesus said about the poor, hoping that they would be motivated by those stories to consider their own lifestyles, spending choices and priorities. It was intriguing, if not a little frustrating, to watch and listen as these young, mostly professional, white Christians identified themselves with the poor in those stories, rather than (for example) with the rich young ruler. Perhaps those of us from 'low power distance' cultures, and those with power in 'high power distance' contexts, sometimes unconsciously co-opt these stories to reinforce our own power by (wrongly) identifying with the powerless in the biblical narratives. In so doing we justify the personal power that we have, camouflaging it from ourselves, to prevent us having to face up to the real import of what these stories tell us.

In situations of diversity, Law comments:

power analysis becomes critical if we are to live out the fullness of the gospel. We must ask the questions: In this social,

[9] Eric Law, *The Wolf shall Dwell with the Lamb: A Spirituality for Leadership in a Multicultural Community* (St Louis, Missouri: Chalice Press, 1993), p. 41.

economic and political context, who has power and who has not? Who is perceived to be powerful and who is perceived to be powerless? In a multicultural world, we might find ourselves shifting back and forth between being powerful and powerless depending on the contexts in which we relate to others. In any given situation, we must determine where we stand in relation to others in the power continuum.[10]

And in such contexts those who have the power must be encouraged and enabled to give it up. This is a refrain that comes through time and again in the New Testament, and is embodied most clearly in Jesus Christ:

> Your attitude should be the same as that of Christ Jesus:
> Who, being in very nature God,
> > did not consider equality with God something to be grasped,
> > but made himself nothing,
> > taking the very nature of a servant,
> > being made in human likeness.
> And being found in appearance as a man,
> > he humbled himself
> > and became obedient to death – even death on a cross!

> (Philippians 2:5–8)

So the first approach toward genuine diversity is based on power analysis, which identifies those who are perceived to have the most power in a given situation, and the surrender of that power for the sake of others. The desire to use power to do good is a tempting one, but benevolent dictators rarely stay benevolent. This temptation was recognized by the author J.R.R. Tolkien, whose epic *The Lord of the Rings* includes the response by the wizard Gandalf to Frodo's offer of the Ring: 'Do not tempt me, Frodo! I dare

---

[10] Ibid., pp. 57–8.

not take it. Not even to keep it safe. I would use this ring from a desire to do good, but through me it would wield a power too great and terrible to imagine.'[11]

Know thyself, grasshopper

Although all humans are unique within their own culture, each national group tends to have certain characteristics which can enrich a team. Brazilian vibrancy, Korean zeal, South African commitment, and American organisation can complement each other to make the combined unit much stronger than the individual parts.[12]

A second important task in any approach that seeks to make diversity an asset rather than a problem is to ensure that there is a good understanding of the different contributions that each one brings. This would be so much easier if there were a standard transferable formula that applied to all such situations. Unfortunately, life is never that simple. As Sue Canney Davison notes:

Each team is unique. High performance cannot be captured in a ready-made formula for how to create synthesis between imaginary French, Japanese, Taiwanese and Russian team members. High performance is created through channelling the forces at play.[13]

---

[11] Dialogue from the 2001 film *The Lord of the Rings: The Fellowship of the Ring*.

[12] Greenlee, 'The Potential and Pitfalls of Multicultural Mission Teams', p. 400.

[13] Sue Canney Davison, 'Creating a High Performance International Team' in Sheila M. Puffer, *Management across Cultures: Insights from Fiction and Practice* (Oxford: Blackwell, 1996), p. 430.

Nonetheless, we can at least derive some preliminary benefit from the considerable amount of work done to identify the general characteristics of different national and generational cultures, even if we have to also include the proviso offered by the authors of the above quotation relating to Brazilian, Korean, South African and American cultural generalizations:

> We know that all missionaries from these countries will not act precisely in the ways we suggest. In fact, descriptions of normal behaviour for a given culture tend to apply only in a general way to the group, not specifically to any individual.[14]

Outlined on the following pages are summaries of some of the most helpful work done in this area, along with the sources of that information for those who want to look into it further. They are, of course, not definitive, nor can they be applied to every person from a given culture, but they do provide useful models.

---

[14] Greenlee, 'The Potential and Pitfalls of Multicultural Mission Teams', p. 399.

Geert Hofstede

Hofstede identified five different dimensions of national cultures. Each national culture can be situated somewhere along the axis of each dimension. The five dimensions he identified are:

Power Distance: the extent to which less powerful members of that culture accept that power is distributed unequally (i.e. the distance between those who have power and those who do not). This dimension reflects inequality, accepted from below, not imposed from above. Power distance is high in Latin, Asian and African countries and low in Germanic, Scandinavian and Anglo-Saxon nations.

Individualism–Collectivism: the extent to which individuals are integrated into groups or not. Individualism prevails in Western and other developed countries and collectivism is common in Eastern and less developed countries. Japan takes a middle position in this dimension.

Masculinity–Femininity: this refers not so much to gender roles as to the degree of emphasis in a culture on success, achievement and assertiveness or caring, modesty and inclusiveness. The former is held to reflect male values and the latter female values. Masculinity is high in Japan, Germanic countries and moderately so in Anglo-Saxon countries. It is low in Scandinavia and the Netherlands and moderately low in some Latin and Asian countries like France, Spain and Thailand.

Uncertainty Avoidance: a society's tolerance for uncertainty and ambiguity. Uncertainty-avoiding cultures minimize the possibility of novel or unstructured situations through strict laws and rules, safety and security measures, and a philosophical/religious commitment to the concept of absolute truth. They are motivated by inner nervous energy and are more emotional.

Uncertainty-accepting cultures are more tolerant of different opinions, reflective and phlegmatic. Latin and Germanic countries and Japan are high in uncertainty avoidance; Chinese, Scandinavian and Anglo-Saxon countries are more uncertainty accepting.

Long-Term or Short-Term Orientation: this deals with the issue of virtue. Long-term cultures value thrift and perseverance; short-term cultures value tradition, the fulfilment of social obligations and protecting one's 'face' or honour. A long-term orientation is associated with East Asian countries and Hofstede notes that their recent economic success has been built on this.

For further information go to < www.geerthofstede.com >. Geert Hofstede, *Culture's Consequences: Comparing Values, Behaviours, Institutions and Organisations across Nations* (London: Corwin Press, 2001).

Charles Hampden-Turner and Fons Trompenaars

These researchers take a similar approach to Hofstede, locating national cultures along six different axes. Some of these are similar to Hofstede's categories; others are different.

Universalism–Particularism: universalist cultures emphasis rules, laws and generalizations; particularist cultures consider the exceptions, special circumstances and obligations created by relationships. Their classic expression of this axis is to ask what you would do if you were in a car being driven by a friend who hits a pedestrian. Universalist cultures (such as Anglo-Saxon and Germanic countries) would not expect you to testify that he or she was driving at a slower speed than he or she actually was; in particularist cultures (such as Russia, China, and India) there would be more expectation that you would.

Individualism–Communitarianism: this category is similar to that of Hofstede, with a respective emphasis on self-achievement, or the achievement of goals and objectives within a community framework.

Specificity–Diffusion: the degree to which one concentrates on the specifics or the whole, the immediate or the context. Specificity emphasizes distinct roles, whereas diffuse cultures see little distinction between the public and private worlds. In Ilyas Halil's story 'No One to Yell At'[15] the Turkish manager (diffuse) working in Montreal doesn't understand why his Canadian employee (specific) scowls when she is sent out to buy two Turkish coffees for him and a client.

---

[15] Halil, 'No One to Yell At', p. 36.

Achieved Status—Ascribed Status: achievement cultures judged you on your own personal record of achievement ('What did you study?'); ascription cultures judge you on birth, kinship and connections ('Where did you study?').

Inner Direction—Outer Direction: are you motivated by inner convictions and conscience or by the example and influence of others? Does one seek to control and change one's environment, or adapt and flow with it? It is no surprise that boxing grew out of inner-directed cultures, whereas judo (where one seeks to use one's opponent's weight and momentum in achieving a throw) emerged from an outer-directed context.

Sequential Time or Synchronous Time: sequential time is an arrow, whereas synchronous time is a circle. In the former case, 'time is money'; in the latter, 'timing is everything'. National cultures that tend to a sequential view of time include Turkey, India and the United States, whereas Hong Kong, Israel and South Korea approximate more closely to the latter.

For further information go to < www.thtconsulting.com >. Charles Hampden-Turner and Fons Trompenaars, *Building Cross-cultural Competence: How to Create Wealth from Conflicting Values* (Chichester: John Wiley, 2000).

Richard Lewis

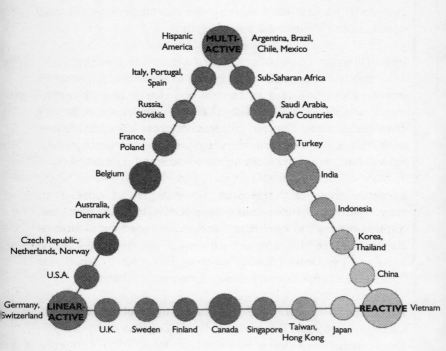

Lewis does not classify national cultures along a series of bilateral axes. Instead he identifies three different types of culture and then locates different national cultures in relation to those three basic types, as below:

Linear-Active Cultures ('*one thing at a time*'): These are task-oriented cultures, which see themselves as efficient, focusing on getting the job done within the scheduled time. Time is linear and clock-related. Their strengths are found in economy of discussion and a focus on the matter at hand. Their weakness is that they can be too fact-oriented, with insufficient focus on people.

Multi-Active Cultures ('jugglers'): People from these cultures are flexible and feel more fulfilled when doing several things at once. They see no reason why various tasks cannot overlap. Time is event- and person-related, and not something that human beings should be dominated by. These cultures are good at (eventually) finding all-embracing solutions and thinking laterally. They can, however, be too random, too argumentative, and generate too many ideas.

Reactive Cultures ('listeners'): These cultures emphasize concentrated listening followed by silent reflection before finally formulating their own thoughts. Discussion is undertaken through a spiral of monologues, and utterances are often incomplete, relying on the listener to interpret their meaning. They enable the development of all-round agreement, but communication can be unclear, and decision making is often a slow process.

For more information go to < www.crossculture.com >, < www.cultureactive.com >.
Richard D. Lewis, *When Cultures Collide: Managing Successfully across Cultures* (London: Nicholas Brealey, 1996).

The above examples all relate to diversity of national culture. Other scales of diversity exist, for example, in relation to generational culture.[16] In all such models, their value lies in providing us with frameworks by which we can understand and adapt to the words and actions of those who are different from ourselves. They are not blueprints that apply in all situations, but they do serve a function in alerting us to anticipate such differences.

Another form of diversity that we have been looking at in this book, but which has not yet been referred to in this chapter, is the expanding diversity of the 'means' of missionary involvement. Programmes undertaken by churches, or by individuals within churches, sometimes in association with a mission agency and sometimes not, are an increasing feature of the contemporary Western missionary movement. The rise in short-term mission, to the extent that it is now more or less 'the new long-term' (i.e. the most common way of being involved in mission), raises questions about how the input of people involved in such programmes can be helped to have a useful impact, rather than simply diverting longer-term personnel into 'child-minding' roles. I would suggest that a new kind of missionary role, that of a 'multi-active' liaison person, might need to be more widely employed. Such a person would have a good understanding of a given local context and its needs, a well-planned but flexible mission strategy, good juggling skills and the temperament and ability to spend his or her energies supporting and facilitating the many and diverse contributions of others into a (semi-)coherent whole. He or she would not see the activities of churches and short-termers as unhelpful distractions from his or her work; instead his or her work would consist of serving those groups and helping them to fit it into a broader context.

[16] See, for example, < www.fourthturning.com > and < www.growingupdigital.com >.

All together now

So we have identified that two key elements of managing diversity are to understand the distinctive needs and outlook of each member of a diverse group and to pay special emphasis to the power dynamics that are operating at any given time. However, even more may be needed.

> Cultural tolerance is only the prerequisite, the necessary condition, of a balanced organisation. Much more, of a positive nature, is needed to link the cultures ... the more differentiation there is between the people, the work, ideologies and time-horizons of different parts of an organisation, the more methods of integration are needed ... Bridges range from copies of correspondence, through joint committees, to coordinating individuals, liaison groups or project teams. In between them are the temporary bridges of task forces, study groups or 'confrontation meetings' between the arguing groups.[17]

This suggests that formal processes need to be established within an organization if diversity is really to be an asset, rather than simply hoping it will be if we talk about it enough. Examples of best practice in this area include:[18]

1. The development of formal procedures, with human and financial resources devoted to any diversity management programme. Diversity is seen as an integrated, ongoing and measurable strategy within an organization.

---

[17] Handy, *Gods of Management*, pp. 99–100.

[18] Taken from Neil Reichenberg, 'Best Practices in Diversity Management', International Personnel Management Association report to the United Nations Expert Group Meeting on Managing Diversity, 3–4 May 2001. Available at < unpan1.un. org/intradoc/groups/public/documents/un/unpan 000715.pdf >.

2. Diversity training is provided, to help personnel to understand the different perspectives created by national and generational cultures, for example.

3. Recruitment, development and retention strategies are seen as central to organizational performance. This creates an environment where personnel diversity is not seen as a marginal luxury but central to an organization's future.

4. Affirmative action programmes are implemented to ensure that personnel diversity reflects the whole potential recruitment pool.

5. Diversity plans are decentralized, though accountable to a central review body.

Regardless of the procedures adopted, what is underlined by these practices is that diversity is an asset to be 'leveraged'. A diverse workforce will not automatically generate the kind of creativity and problem solving that it is able to do; it can also remain divided and breed misunderstanding. Genuine diversity can be a useful resource in a complex and changing environment, but we must not assume it 'just happens'. Even the earliest history of Christianity shows us that it is something to be worked at.

> We who are strong ought to bear with the failings of the weak and not to please ourselves. Each of us should please his neighbour for his good, to build him up
>
> (Romans 15:1–2).

> Before certain men came from James, he [Peter] used to eat with the Gentiles. But when they arrived, he began to draw back and separate himself from the Gentiles because he was afraid of those who belonged to the circumcision group
>
> (Galatians 2:12).

He himself is our peace, who has made the two one and has destroyed the barrier, the dividing wall of hostility ...

(Ephesians 2:14).

Even Paul and the other apostles had to work hard, to teach and to write to the early Christian communities, to ensure that the church did not remain a culturally monolithic Jewish sect. A nationally, generationally and organizationally diverse future is forcing itself upon us whether we like it or not. It may not be easy to get the best from it, but live in it we must.

Bibliography

Achebe, Chinua, 'Named for Victoria, Queen of England' in Ashcroft, B., Griffiths, Gareth and Tiffin, Helen, *The Postcolonial Studies Reader* (London: Routledge, 1995)

Anderson, Allan, 'Structures and Patterns in Pentecostal Mission', unpublished paper given at the Wisdom in Mission forum, Alresford, Hants, UK, 14–15 May 2002

Anderson, Rufus, *The Time for the World's Conversion Come* (1837)

Ansari, Khizar Humayun and Jackson, June, *Managing Cultural Diversity at Work* (London: Kogan Page, 1995)

Ashcroft, B., Griffiths, Gareth and Tiffin, Helen, *The Postcolonial Studies Reader* (London: Routledge, 1995)

Bahloul, Mongi, 'English in Carthage, or The Tenth Crusade' a paper given at the PostColonialismS/PoliticalCorrectnesseS conference, Casablanca, Morocco, 12–14 April 2001. Available at < www.victorianweb.org/post/poldiscourse/casablanca/program.html >

Baker, Dwight P., 'William Carey and the Business Model for Mission' (2002). Available at < www.globalconnections.co.uk/business.asp >

Barber, Benjamin, 'Jihad vs McWorld', *The Atlantic Monthly* (March 1992)

Barlow, John Perry, 'The Next Economy of Ideas: Will Copyright Survive the Napster Bomb?', *Wired* (October 2000)

Baudrillard, Jean, 'Simulacra and Simulations' in Poster, Mark (ed.), *Jean Baudrillard: Selected Writings* (Stanford: Stanford University Press, 1988). Available at < www.stanford.edu/dept/HPS/Baudrillard/Baudrillard_Simulacra.html >

Bauman, Zygmunt, *Globalization: The Human Consequences* (Cambridge: Polity Press, 1998)

———, *Liquid Modernity* (Cambridge: Polity Press, 2000)

Bedell, Geraldine, 'The Changing Face of the Brand', *The Observer* Review section, 19 January 2003. Available at < www.observer.co.uk/review/story/0,6903,877476,00.html >

Bergquist, William, *The Postmodern Organization: Mastering the Art of Irreversible Change* (San Francisco: Jossey-Bass, 1993)

Berger, Peter L. and Huntington, Samuel P., *Many Globalizations: Cultural Diversity in the Contemporary World* (New York: Oxford University Press, 2002)

Bosch, David, *Transforming Mission* (Maryknoll, New York: Orbis, 1991)

Brandström, Per, 'Who is a Sukuma and Who is a Nyamwezi? Ethnic Identity in West-Central Tanzania', Working Papers in African Studies #27, Department of Cultural Anthropology, University of Uppsala (1986)

Brathwaite, Edward Kamau, 'Creolization in Jamaica' in Ashcroft, B., Griffiths, Gareth and Tiffin, Helen, *The Postcolonial Studies Reader* (London: Routledge, 1995)

Canney Davison, Sue, 'Creating a High Performance International Team' in Puffer, Sheila M., *Management across Cultures: Insights from Fiction and Practice* (Oxford: Blackwell, 1996)

Carey, William, 'An Enquiry into the Obligation of Christians to Use Means for the Conversion of the Heathens' (1792) in Winter, Ralph D. and Hawthorne, Stephen C. (eds), *Perspectives on the World Christian Movement* (Carlisle: Paternoster Press, 1992^2)

Carson, Don (ed.), *The Church in the Bible and the World* (Exeter: Paternoster, 1987)

Caulkin, Simon, 'Mission Impossible', *The Observer* Business section, 25 July 1999

———, 'Thinking Outside the Box', *The Observer*, 26 May 2002. Available at < www.observer.co.uk/business/story/0,6903,72 2116,00.html >

Chester, Tim, 'Christ's Little Flock: Towards an Ecclesiology of the Cross', *Evangel* 19/1 (Spring 2001), pp. 13–21

Conn, Harvey, 'Contextual Theologies: The Problem of Agendas', *Evangelical Review of Theology* 15/3 (1989)

Coupland, Douglas, *Life after God* (London: Simon & Schuster, 1994)

——, *Microserfs* (London: Flamingo, 1995)

——, *Miss Wyoming* (London: Flamingo, 2000)

Davison, Sue Canney, 'Creating a High Performance International Team', in Puffer, Sheila M., *Management Across Cultures: Insights from Fiction and Practice* (Oxford: Blackwell, 1996)

Engel, James F. and Dyrness, William A., *Changing the Mind of Missions: Where have we Gone Wrong?* (Downers Grove, Illinois: InterVarsity Press, 2000)

Engel, Richard, 'Inside Al-Qaeda: A Window into the World of Militant Islam and the Afghan Alumni' (2001). Available at < www.janes.com/security/international_security/news/misc/janes010928_1_n.shtml >

Finnström, Sverker, 'Postcoloniality and the Postcolony: Theories of the Global and the Local', Working Paper on Anthropology #7, University of Uppsala, Sweden (1997). Available at < 65.107.211.206/post/poldiscourse/finnstrom/finnstrom2. html >

Forster, E.M., *Howards End* (Harmondsworth: Penguin, 2000)

Fukuyama, Francis, 'The End of History?', *The National Interest* 16 (Summer 1989)

Gladwell, Malcolm, *The Tipping Point* (London: Little, Brown, 2000)

Goudzwaard, Bob, *Globalization and the Kingdom of God* (Grand Rapids, Michigan: Baker, 2001)

Green, Stanley W., 'How Mennonites Repositioned a Traditional Mission', *International Bulletin of Missionary Research* 23/4 (October 1999)

Greenlee, David, Cho, Yong Joong and Thulare, Abraham, 'The Potential and Pitfalls of Multicultural Mission Teams' in O'Donnell, Kelly (ed.), *Doing Member Care Well: Perspectives and Practices from around the World* (Pasadena, California: William Carey Library, 2002)

Gross, Leonard, 'Sixteenth-Century Hutterian Mission' in Shenk, Wilbert (ed.), *Anabaptism and Mission* (Scottdale, Pennsylvania: Herald Press, 1984)

Gutting, G., *The Cambridge Companion to Foucault* (Cambridge: Cambridge University Press, 1994)

Halil, Ilyas, 'No One to Yell At' in Halil, Ilyas, *Unregulated Chicken Butts and Other Stories* (Salt Lake City, Utah: University of Utah Press, 1990)

Hampden-Turner, Charles and Trompenaar, Fons, *Building Cross-cultural Competence: How to Create Wealth from Conflicting Values* (Chichester: John Wiley, 2000)

Handy, Charles, *The Empty Raincoat* (New York: Random House, 1995)

——, *Gods of Management: The Changing Work of Organisations* (London: Arrow, 1995)

Hannigan, John, 'Fantasy Cities', *New Internationalist* 308 (December 1998)

Held, David, McGrew, Anthony, Goldblatt, David and Perraton, Jonathan, *Global Transformations* (Cambridge: Polity, 1999)

Hertz, Noreena, *The Silent Takeover* (London: Heinemann, 2001)

Heslam, Peter, *Globalization: Unravelling the New Capitalism* (Cambridge: Grove, 2002)

Hirst, P. and Thompson, G., *Globalization in Question: The International Economy and the Possibilities of Governance* (Cambridge: Polity Press, 1996)

Hofstede, Geert, *Culture's Consequences: Comparing Values, Behaviours, Institutions and Organisations across Nations* (London: Corwin Press, 2001)

Hope, Jeremy and Hope, Tony, *Competing in the Third Wave* (Boston, Massachusetts: Harvard Business School Press, 1997)

Horne, Melvill, *Letters on Missions, Addressed to the Protestant Ministers of the British Churches* (Bristol, 1794)

Hughes, Dewi, *Castrating Culture: A Christian Perspective on Ethnic Identity from the Margins* (Carlisle: Paternoster Press, 2001)

Huntington, Samuel P., 'The Clash of Civilisations?', *Foreign Affairs* 72/3 (1993)

Ingleby, Jonathan, 'Trickling Down or Shaking the Foundations: Is Contextualization Neutral?', *Missiology* 25/2 (April 1997)

Jeffrey, Tim, *Connect!* (Carlisle: Paternoster/Spring Harvest, 2003)

Kaplan, Robert, 'The Coming Anarchy', *The Atlantic Monthly* (February 1994)

Kelly, Gerard (1999), *Get a Grip on the Future without Losing your Hold on the Past* (London: Monarch, 1999)

Klein, Naomi, *No Logo* (London: HarperCollins, 2000)

——, 'Out of the Ordinary', *The Guardian* Weekend Magazine, 25 January 2003

Law, Eric, *The Wolf shall Dwell with the Lamb: A Spirituality for Leadership in a Multicultural Community* (St Louis, Missouri: Chalice Press, 1993)

Leadbeater, Charles, *Up the Down Escalator* (London: Viking, 2002)

Lewis, Richard D., *When Cultures Collide: Managing Successfully across Cultures* (London: Nicholas Brealey, 1996)

Lundy, David, *We are the World: Globalisation and the Changing Face of Missions* (Carlisle: OM, 1999)

MacFhionnlaigh, Fearghas, 'Creative Tensions', *Scottish Bulletin of Evangelical Theology* 14/1 (Spring 1996)

Malherbe, Abraham J., *Social Aspects of Early Christianity* (Philadelphia: Fortress Press, 1983[2])

Márquez, Gabriel García, 'One of these Days' in Márquez, Gabriel García, *No One Writes to the Colonel and Other Stories*, Bernstein, J. S. (tr.) (London: Harper & Row, 1968)

Middleton, J. Richard and Walsh, Brian J., *Truth is Stranger than it Used to Be: Biblical Faith in a Postmodern Age* (London: SPCK, 1997)

Moynagh, Michael, *Changing World, Changing Church* (London: Monarch, 2001)

Neill, Stephen, *A History of Christian Missions* (London: Penguin, 1986[2])

O'Brien, Peter, 'The Church as a Heavenly and Eschatological Entity' in Carson, Don (ed.), *The Church in the Bible and the World* (Exeter: Paternoster, 1987), pp. 88–119

O'Donnell, Kelly (ed.), *Doing Member Care Well: Perspectives and Practices from around the World* (Pasadena, California: William Carey Library, 2002)

Ohmae, Kenichi, 'The Rise of the Region State', *Foreign Affairs* 72/2 (1993)

O'Meara, P., Mehlinger, H. and Krain, M. (eds), *Globalization and the Challenges of a New Century: A Reader* (Bloomington, Indiana: Indiana University Press, 2000)

Orwell, George, *1984* (Harmondsworth: Penguin, 1967)

Patton, Cornelius, *The Business of Missions* (New York: Macmillan, 1924)

Peters, Tom, *Thriving on Chaos* (London/New York: HarperCollins, 1987)

Poster, Mark (ed.), *Jean Baudrillard: Selected Writings* (Stanford: Stanford University Press, 1988)

Powell, Mike, *Information Management for Development Organisations* (Oxford: Oxfam, 1999)

Puffer, Sheila M., *Management across Cultures: Insights from Fiction and Practice* (Oxford: Blackwell, 1996)

Putnam, Robert D., 'Bowling Alone: America's Declining Social Capital', *Journal of Democracy* 6/1 (January 1995). Available at < muse.jhu.edu/demo/journal_of_democracy/v006/putnam.html >

——, *Bowling Alone: The Collapse and Revival of American Community* (New York: Touchstone, 2001)

——, 'Let's Play Together', *The Observer*, 25 March 2001. Available at < www.observer.co.uk/comment/story/0,6903,462665,00.html >

Rajgopal, S., Venkatachalam, M. and Kotha, S., 'The Value-Relevance of Network Advantages: The Case of E-commerce Firms', *Journal of Accounting Research* (December 2002). Available at < faculty.fuqua.duke.edu/~rajgopal/bio/files/JAR%202002b.pdf >

Reichenberg, Neil, 'Best Practices in Diversity Management', International Personnel Management Association report to the United Nations Expert Group Meeting on Managing Diversity, 3–4 May 2001. Available at < http://unpan1.un.org/intradoc/groups/public/documents/un/unpan000715.pdf >

Ritzer, George, *The McDonaldization of Society* (Thousand Oaks, California: Pine Forge Press, 1993)

Rushdie, Salman, *Shame* (New York: Vintage, 1984)

Rynkiewich, Michael A., 'The World in my Parish: Rethinking the Standard Missiological Model', *Missiology: An International Review* 30/3 (July 2002), pp. 301–21

Schrage, Michael, 'Network Theory's New Math', *Strategy+ Business Magazine* (fourth quarter 2002). Available at < www. strategy-business.com/press/article/?art=9966476&pg=0 >

Schreiter, Robert J., *The New Catholicity: Theology between the Global and the Local* (Maryknoll, New York: Orbis, 1997)

Shenk, Wilbert (ed.), *Anabaptism and Mission* (Scottdale, Pennsylvania: Herald Press, 1984)

——, *Changing Frontiers of Mission* (Maryknoll, New York: Orbis, 1999)

Sine, Tom, *Mustard Seed Versus McWorld: Reinventing Christian Life* and *Mission for the New Millennium* (Crowborough: Monarch, 1999)

Skreslet, Stanley H., 'Impending Transformation: Mission Structures for a New Century', *International Bulletin of Missionary Research* 23/1 (January 1999)

Skocpol, Theda, 'Unravelling from Above', *The American Prospect* 7/25 (March 1996), pp. 20–25. Available at < www.prospect. org/print/V7/25/25–cnt2.html >

Slavitt, David, 'Name Six Famous Belgians' in Slavitt, David, *Short Stories are not Real Life* (Baton Rouge, Louisiana: Louisiana State University Press, 1991), pp. 43–57

Smith, David, *Mission after Christendom* (London: Darton, Longman & Todd, 2003)

Stambaugh, John and Balch, David, *The Social World of the First Christians* (London: SPCK, 1986)

Tan, Kang San (OMF Malaysia), 'Interview', *Global Connections Newsletter* (September 2002)

Taves, Scott, 'Find Your Sole Mate', *Wired* (January 2003)

Tayeb, Monir, *The Management of a Multicultural Workforce* (Chichester: John Wiley & Sons, 1996)

Taylor, William D. (ed.), *The Iguassu Dialogue: Global Missiology for the 21st Century* (Grand Rapids, Michigan: Baker, 2000)

Tidball, Derek, *An Introduction to the Sociology of the New Testament* (Exeter: Paternoster, 1983)

Tiplady, Richard, 'Let X = X: Generation X and World Mission' in Taylor, William D. (ed.), *The Iguassu Dialogue: Global Missiology for the 21ˢᵗ Century* (Grand Rapids, Michigan: Baker, 2000), pp. 463–75

Toffler, Alvin, *The Third Wave* (London: Pan, 1981)

Toynbee, Polly, 'A Whole Nation of Meldrews: I Just Can't Believe It', *The Guardian*, 28 August 2002. Available at < www.guardian.co.uk/comment/story/0,3604,781684,00.html >

Valerio, Ruth, 'Globalisation and the Poor: Tearfund Policy Paper' (2002). Available at < www.globalconnections.co.uk/pdfs/globalization.pdf >

Walls, Andrew, *The Missionary Movement in Christian History* (Edinburgh: T. & T. Clark, 1996)

——, 'Old Athens and New Jerusalem', *International Bulletin of Missionary Research* 21/4 (October 1997)

Waters, Malcolm, *Globalization* (London: Routledge, 2001²)

Winter, Ralph D., 'The Two Structures of God's Redemptive Mission' in Winter, Ralph D. and Hawthorne, Steven C. (eds), *Perspectives on the World Christian Movement* (Carlisle: Paternoster, 1992²)

——, and Hawthorne, Stephen C. (eds), *Perspectives on the World Christian Movement* (Carlisle: Paternoster Press, 1992²)

Wirth, Karl, 'Of the Making of Many Meetings there is no End: Or, How I Learned to Stop Going to Bible Study and Love Non-Christians', *Re:Generation Quarterly* 7/2 (Summer 2001)

Wright, Chris, *Deuteronomy* (NIBC; Carlisle: Paternoster, 1996)

Zemke, Ron, Raines, Claire and Filipczak, Bob, *Generations at Work* (New York: AMACOM, 2000)

van der Zijpp, N., 'From Anabaptist Missionary Congregation to Mennonite Seclusion' in Shenk, Wilbert (ed.), *Anabaptism and Mission* (Scottdale, Pennsylvania: Herald Press, 1984), pp. 119–36

Index